"Unconsc

Freeing the Body

by

Brown Landone

A COURSE OF 16 LESSONS

MW01282676

Issued by

The Landone Foundation

Orlando, Florida

KESSINGER PUBLISHING'S
RARE MYSTICAL REPRINTS

THOUSANDS OF SCARCE BOOKS
ON THESE AND OTHER SUBJECTS:

Freemasonry * Akashic * Alchemy * Alternative Health * Ancient Civilizations * Anthroposophy * Astrology * Astronomy * Aura * Bible Study * Cabalah * Cartomancy * Chakras * Clairvoyance * Comparative Religions * Divination * Druids * Eastern Thought * Egyptology * Esoterism * Essenes * Etheric * ESP * Gnosticism * Great White Brotherhood * Hermetics * Kabalah * Karma * Knights Templar * Kundalini * Magic * Meditation * Mediumship * Mesmerism * Metaphysics * Mithraism * Mystery Schools * Mysticism * Mythology * Numerology * Occultism * Palmistry * Pantheism * Parapsychology * Philosophy * Prosperity * Psychokinesis * Psychology * Pyramids * Qabalah * Reincarnation * Rosicrucian * Sacred Geometry * Secret Rituals * Secret Societies * Spiritism * Symbolism * Tarot * Telepathy * Theosophy * Transcendentalism * Upanishads * Vedanta * Wisdom * Yoga * *Plus Much More!*

DOWNLOAD A FREE CATALOG
AND
SEARCH OUR TITLES AT:

www.kessinger.net

C O N T E N T S

UNCONSCIOUS FREEING OF THE BODY

by

Brown Landone

NON-CONSCIOUS MUSCLE ACTIVITY - LESSON I

Life - if you allowed it to be lived according to the spirit of your soul - would mean ideal completeness of body structure and ideal perfection of activity of every tissue and organ of the body.

But when conscious mind interferes with free expression of spirit, in and through the body, then the body suffers all the ills due to being shut off from the full energy of spirit.

And NOTHING BUT conscious mind ever interferes!

This is supremely important, - because (1) free expression of spirit is life; and (2) repression by conscious mind, is death.

Spirit in free expression might double the years of man's body. But conscious mind, starts the slowing dying process, as soon as results of its repression have accumulated enough, to begin to affect the brain centers through which energies of the body, manifest.

And even while living under repressed conditions of mind, man can not fully enjoy life, because of lack of energy, lack of buoyancy, lack of vitality, lack of freedom from illness, lessening youthfulness, and increasing age of body.

At first you may think that many ills of body, and lessened activities of its tissues and organs, are due mainly to the lack of proper food, or to lack of sufficient exercise, or lack of breathing freely and fully, or lack of elimination, et cetera.

But all of these are SECONDARY results - NOT primal causes.

The basic primal CAUSE of all mis-activities, and all lack of activity and all lessened activity, IS repression by conscious mind!

I repeat emphatically: the only reason there is ANY suppression of normal free activity in life, is that conscious mind RESTRICTS its expression!

Such suppressive restriction begins very early in childhood. Even material means are used - mothers give soothing syrups to babies to quiet their crying, or to calm their restlessness. Yet the crying is essential both for development of the child's breathing capacity, and for supply of more blood to expand the brain.

And every impulse of restlessness is due either to some restricted condition enforced on the child, or to impulses of activity
within the brain centers - impulses which long for freer expression,
to lead to greater development of tissues and organs

<u>Than there is repression of the mind of the child!</u>
As it grows, it is cautioned - commanded - compelled - <u>NOT</u> to
<u>DO</u> this, or not to do that - all because conscious mind 'thinks' it
<u>Is</u> not the proper thing to do.
And later - and very soon in life - there come commands <u>NOT</u> to
<u>FEEL</u> this or that; even not to think this or that.

And each such repression of action or feeling - or impulsive
expanding desire of the soul - <u>IS</u> <u>due</u> <u>to</u> <u>conscious</u> <u>mind.</u>

Hence the body - born to be the means of freely expressing a
soul of spirit, soon becomes so bound by chains of conscious mind,
that freedom of expression is seldom regained in later life.

This affects health: It may be that every mis-functioning and
lack of functioning of the entire digestive and entire eliminative
system is primarily due to repressed impulses of free elimination
at the time elimination should take place.

And every repression of an impulse freely to express the normal
activity of the emotional nature, results in reaction on heart and
lungs and liver and pancreas - and most deadly of all - on the
endocrine glands, the very masters of life in the body.

In contrast, - spirit - manifesting freely <u>through</u> body - results
in attaining of limitless freedom of body and soul;

<u>Many</u> <u>methods</u> of freeing the body, have been tried by those who
have reached the years of understanding, and realize how greatly their
repressions of the past have hindered the joy of life, and even
caused ills and diseases of the body.

Many methods have been tried <u>by</u> <u>the</u> <u>conscious</u> <u>mind</u> to free the
body, - for when conditions became too bad even conscious mind
tries to relieve the very ills it has caused.

Yet it has never yet been able to do so, <u>because</u> conscious
mind can never give up its repressing nature, even in trying to
relieve conditions of its own repression.

This course is written - to give you a <u>NON-</u> conscious means of
freeing the body so completely, that soul may express in fullness -
fulfilling the desire of the heart for perfection of the structure
and perfection of activity.

UNCONSCIOUS FREEING OF THE BODY

by

Brown Landone

INNER AND OUTER MUSCLES - LESSON II

The worst of all the thousands of ills produced in the body, **BY** repression and suppression of the activity of spirit of the soul, **IS** the tensity of the INNER muscles of the body

When inner muscles are tensed, they clamp down on nerves and prevent free flow of energy - thus shutting off energy to this or that organ or tissue of the body, or even to the entire body itself.

Let me define for you, the term inner muscles, and what we mean by it, as distinct from outer muscles.

The words 'inner' and 'outer' are not technical terms at all. Yet I use them, because they WILLhelp you clearly to understand what I mean.

By OUTER muscles I mean the muscles of your arms or legs, or the outer muscles of your neck or your chest or your torso. Outer muscles are those which you can MOVE by voluntary action - that is, by intending to move them.

For example, if you wish to reach for a pencil, your intention automatically directs the muscles of your arm and hand and fingers to reach for the pencil.

These outer muscles are controlled BY your conscious mind.

By INNER muscles, I mean all muscles - large or small - whose action you can NOT control by your conscious mind!

That is, muscles along the inside of the back up and down the spine; muscle fibers of the heart, and of the stomach and intestinal walls, and of every other internal organ of the body.

Also by inner muscles, I include all the muscle fibers of all the wrappings of all the nerves or nerve ganglia of the body. And all the muscle fibers - tens of millions of them - controlling extention or contraction of all the blood tubes.

These tiny muscle fibers of blood tubes are important! Your very life OR death depends on them! By distention or contraction of the size of blood tubes, they regulate the balanced or unbalanced flow of blood to and from all organs of the body.

Hence, they also control the blood flow to brain centers!

When the blood flow to brain centers is lessened, then the activity and energy of that brain center is reduced.

Then every organ supplied by energy from that brain center is depleted. This may result only in greatly lessened activity, or even in shrinking of the organ, lessening its size as well as vitality.

On a balanced blood flow, depend the life and activity of sex organs, their continuing activity, their size and vitality.

Then also normal blood flow is essential for the health and activity of the mysterious endocrine glands!

So on the balance of blood flow, life itself depends!

Often inner tensity effects the tiny muscles of throat and larynx - preventing production of beautiful voice tones.

There INNER muscles can become MUCH MORE TENSE, and much more continuously, and detrimentally tense than outer muscles.

They often close down on sheaths of nerves and even on nerve ganglia or brain centers, and hinder nerve action and the flow of all energy in the related organs and tissues.

Remember that these inner muscles can be tensed much more than the outer muscles of your body can be tensed.

The intense tensity of an outer muscle you call a cramp.
And you know how very painful such a cramp is - in your foot, or in the calf of your leg, or in the side muscles of the torso.

Now imagine such a cramp CONTINUING for ten YEARS!

This often happens in case of the inner muscles, because they are not consciously controlled, and there are NO specialized nerve fibers of 'feeling' in such inner muscles, and hence they do not report the pain of such a cramp to your conscious mind.

So when they are tensed and working all sorts of ills, you usually do nothing to free them and do not even realize that many conditions from which you suffer are due to such tensities.

But whether their cramping is reported or not - so that you know it consciously - the very detrimental effects are produced and continue as long as they are tensed.

UNCONSCIOUS FREEING OF THE BODY

by

Brown Landone

THE HOSTS OF ILLS - EASILY REMEDIED - LESSON III

All joys you lack in life are due to lack of expression.

Lack of expression is always due to repression, which usually begins with such tensing of the inner muscles, that soul can not manifest through the body, freely and fully.

Perhaps the best way to summarize briefly some of the ill effects, produced later in life by inner muscle tensity, is to start with a few of those which occur in the head, and then list several of the ills that result from inner tensity - plane by plane - down through the body, even to the feet.

One of most serious results is on the brains of the body.

In the body there are:
(1) Four major brains - one on the head; three in the torso;
(2) Thousands of areas of each of these brains;
(3) Millions of brain centers of each of these areas; and
(4) Hundreds of millions of brain cell groups throughout the body and every tissue!

Every tissue - even your arm muscles - is shot through with millions of tiny brains, each charged with electronic energy.

It is not necessary for me to tell you that brain tissues are composed of cells which are some of the most finely organized and delicately functioning cells of the entire body.

For example, the small brain center of sight is a telephone exchange. From it, 160,000,000 wires run out, to carry messages through their inter-locking substations to all portions of the brain and to every organ of the body.

Now let's merely list some of the ill effects of inner muscle tensity - affecting brain structure and brain centers!

Tensity of any muscle in the body changes the blood flow.
That causes a reaction of the flow of blood to the brain.
Then the reaction reacts in the opposite direction.

Then also every mental or emotional stimulation of a brain center, can cause distension and increase of blood in its related part of the body, EVEN THOUGH that part makes NO movement at all.

Fifty years ago these facts were definitely proven by Doctor

Anderson of Yale, who invented the first blood-balance muscle-bed!

This is not a good name for this marvelous apparatus.
It should have been called Blood Flow Indicator!
But it is still called muscle-bed, so I still use the term.
It is now vastly improved - a very delicate mechanism.

Even the old muscle-bed was so delicately balanced, that if
but a few extra drops of blood flowed to the toes, the foot of the
table would tip down.
Or if a little extra blood flowed to the brain, the head of
the table would tip down.
The table could also tip side to side, and diagonally.

When a person - placed on such a muscle-bed - closes his eyes
and for only ten seconds thinks of the thumb of his right hand,
the extra flow of blood to that thumb is great enough - even without
any movement of the thumb itself - to cause the muscle-bed to tip
toward the right side.

So also, whenever any inner muscle is tensed - which means
that its fibers tighten and clamp down on the blood tubes in the
muscle - its fibers squeeze blood out of the muscle, and cause an
unbalanced blood flow in the related brain center.

If such tensity continues - and in an inner muscle it may continue for years - the connected brain center is overflooded with
blood all that time. Then very serious conditions result.

There can be no headache; there can be no pain in the head; there
can be no underfunctioning or overfunctioning of normal activity of
any brain center; there can be no abnormal growth in the brain, -
UNLESS there has been or is, an unbalance of the blood flow to the
portion of the brain in which the ill condition exists.

Before briefly summarizing other conditions resulting from tensity
of inner muscles in other parts of the body, please realize that what
I have written of brain centers, applies to every part of the body, for
every minute portion of the body is supplied by blood tubes.

There can be NO swelling in any part of the body, UNLESS the
blood tubes in that part are distended by extra blood.
The tubes are much larger than their normal size, in the tissues
in which the swelling occurs!
In fact 'swelling' is nothing but gorging of a part with blood.

There can be NO pain in any part of the body, UNLESS there is
swelling of blood tubes.

Pain is caused by swollen blood tubes pressing and pinching

tiny nerve fibers in between the tubes, in the swollen tissue.

Imagine the pressure on nerves in any part of the body when its blood tubes are swollen to three times their normal size.

No wonder the nerves cry out in pain, and beg you to do something to relieve the pressure due to the extra blood.

When you now think of all the organs of the body - from head to feet - it is easy to understand that the tensity of any inner muscle may affect flow of blood in many parts.

Overflow or underflow to ears and eyes and throat and nose, or to lungs and heart, or to liver and kidneys and spleen and pancreas, or to intestines and the sex organs, or to upper limbs or lower limbs - CAN produce abnormal conditions in each or all of these organs or structures - conditions due to too much or too little blood.

There can be NO un-balance of blood flow - other than that caused by a serious accident - EXCEPT that which is produced by internal tensity of INNER or outer muscles.

Tensed outer muscles give up their tensity in a short time.
But the inner muscles may remain tensed for years, unless relieved by UN-CONSCIOUS freeing of the body.

Tensity of inner muscles may be due to any one of many causes!
Strain of life; reaction to emotions; or monotony of life!
Any of these CAN and DOES cause tensity of inner muscles.

But the most frequent and constant cause of such tensity is the continuing - and often increasing - repression of impulses and feelings and activities - almost from the day the child is born, to well along into later life.

Then - in later life - the habit of internal tensity can become so fixed, that it seems impossible to remedy it.
And it is impossible, by all the means usually used!

Yet the remedy IS very simple, IF you use methods which FREE the body FROM control of the "conscious mind" - that is, from continuous restriction of the conscious mind - so that spirit can manifest through the body in fullness and freedom.

It is not difficult to secure the result desired, provided you follow the directions in these Lessons, - to give little conscious attention to what your body may be doing during processes of freeing it UN-consciously or NON-consciously or SUB-consciously.
Not only does tensity of inner muscles produce ill effects on

the organs themselves, but it is the cause of many general results in life - such as lack of vitality and energy, and lack of endurance and lack of youthfulness!

Certainly when inner muscles are tensed in any portion of the body, they react on the nerves; and nerves are the great power lines of the body, which carry spirit energy from brain centers to the organs and tissues to give them life and activity.

And when tensity of inner muscles interferes with the flow of power to your outer muscles, then your whole outer body lacks energy and endurance and power.
Also its activities become limited and restricted!
And its cells often become continuously fatigued!
Then its cells do not reproduce themselves youthfully.

When this inner tensity is continued to such an extent that it even interferes with the blood flow to nerve centers, then you feel inner lifelessness, and completely lack the joy of life.

And these conditions continue, so long as the cause continues. All such fatigue and lack of energy may continue, even though you know that your soul's strength is limitless; and that its power is infinite because it is of spirit and spirit is limitless.

Nevertheless, it does little good for your 'conscious mind,' positively to assert that your soul has limitless energy, when at the same time, the very activity of your conscious mind is tending to produce greater tensity of the inner muscles - resulting in greater blocking of the power lines and making it the more impossible for your soul to express and use its infinite energy.

Putting 'repressive' conscious mind to work to free the body of the repression of conscious mind, is like putting a bank burglar to work robbing banks, in order to stop bank robberies.

Tensity of the inner muscles - caused by the repression OF conscious mind - can not be freed BY repressive conscious mind.

Now that you know something of the results of inner muscle tensity on the blood tubes and nerves, it is easy to understand, that NO abnormal growth could even begin to grow in any organ of the body, UNLESS its perfect blood flow had been hindered and unbalanced for year

Also now it is easy for you to understand, that there can be NO decrease of functioning or activity of eye or ear or any other special sense of the body - or in fact, of any internal organ of the body - unless the flow of energy to that part or organ, had been lessened, either by the tensities caused by repressive restrictions of the conscious mind and by lessened discriminative activity of the part due to the same cause.

I have not, of course, named one tenth of the ill effects that result from inner tensity of inner muscles.

The principal truth to know now, is that such conditions can NOT be relieved by conscious mind, but that they CAN be relieved and freed by NON-conscious freeing of the body - which frees it of the restrictions of conscious mind and lets spirit energy flow through freely.

And again, I emphasize that conscious mind can NOT even attempt to free inner muscles without danger to the body.

Such danger is just as certain as the danger of the conscious attempting to count the molecules of carbonic-acid which flow into the heart, and then trying to regulate the action of the heart to free the body of that poison.

As stated in another Lesson, IF conscious mind should attempt to do this; it would be just about 2,000 years too late in securing the result, for conscious mind would require 2,009 years to do the counting that must be done in four minutes to prevent death!

I use the heart, only to illustrate the difference between (1) activity of spirit, and (2) activity of conscious mind.
And what I write of the heart, is true of every organ.

There can be NO pain or lack of energy in any body part, unless nerves are strangled by pressure of swollen blood.
OR unless nerves are starved because of shrunken blood tubes bringing too little food to the nerves and adjoining tissues.

There can be NO abnormal growth, - unless the tensity of inner muscles has for years pinched blood tubes in one part of the body, so that some other part of the body has been gorged with blood.

Thus at the same time the flow of spirit from the brain is shut off by pinching of the nerves by the swollen tubes.

There is no remedy, except to UN-consciously free the body from the repressed conditions due to the tensity of inner muscles!
That freedom can NOT be effected by conscious mind, - because consciousness always tends to tense muscle fibers of the body, instead of relax them.

FREEDOM can come ONLY by a SPIRIT flowing freely through body - effecting freedom of structure and perfection of free inner activity!

This Lesson does not adequately picture to you the great lack of joy in life, the lack of freedom, and the lack of maintained youthfulness caused by internal tensity.
This Lesson relates mainly to physical ills of repression.

UNCONSCIOUS FREEING OF THE BODY

by

Brown Landone

THE PRIMAL FUNCTIONS OF SOUL IN BODY - LESSON IV

The body is understood more fully as the means of expressing
the powers of the soul, if you know of its three primal functions.

FIRST, there is the function of all brains of the body.

Not only the brain in the skull, but also the three in the
torso, and the tens of millions of little brain cell groups throughout the body - ARE the GENERATORS of spirit.

But the word 'generator' is not a true use of its meaning.
It was mischosen even for its use in electrical science.
It means 'to give birth', and you know that a dynamo NEVER gives
birth to electricity, any more than your radio 'gives birth' to sound.

Instead of calling brain a generator, we should call it, an
In-Spirer of energy.
The brain centers of the body ARE the inspirers of spirit.
That is, they take-in spirit - the cosmic energy of God.

Then the SECOND basic body function is transmission of energy.

The nerves of the body are its power lines, used by the soul to
transmit itself through the body.

The nerves are great trunk lines, and also tiny power lines, to
carry the in-spired energy of God, TO every tissue of the body.

The THIRD basic function of the body is effected by the muscles,
which are the MOTORS of the body.

The large outer muscles of the body are motors!

Also the little inner muscles - and all tiny muscle fibers
working independently in every organ of the body - work as motors.

These THREE activities ARE the BASIC PRIMAL activities of body!
When they function, they let soul express through body.

Repeat this, to make it very clear.

FIRST, the great brain centers act as IN-spirers of the energy
of the universe - taking-in energy to be used in the body.

Second, tens of millions of nerve trunk lines carry the power, from the brain centers TO the motors.

Third, in all muscle fibers - whether in internal organs or in great outer muscles - there are actual electronic motors, which use the energy of the soul, by turning it into action.

IF NOTHING ever interfered with these three functions, then there would be such perfection of structure and perfection of activity of body throughout life here, that the life of the body would probably continue for from 200 or 300 years.

INTERNAL TENSITY of inner muscles TIGHTENS and presses and crushes blood tubes!
They also crush and pinch nerves!
Thus internal tensity of inner muscles interferes with the free flow of energy in the body, and may even unbalance the activity of brain centers themselves.

Such tensity often completely BLOCKS the flow of energy along the nerve paths!
Also it often freezes the energy to a standstill or stagnant condition IN the motors - either in brain centers, or in the internal organs, or in the great outer muscles.

Tensity of inner muscles is unintentional MURDER.
It first shuts off life energy from a tissue!
Then it greatly reduces its activity!
Next, it destroys its very structure!

Such death of a tissue IS physiological murder!

Unconscious freeing of the body is salvation that results in freedom of spirit, manifesting in ever increasing life.

That which is most mystic to biologists and physiologists is not birth - even though birth is mysterious.
But to the minds of biologists and physiologists, the greatest mystery - the mystic mystery is death!
They cannot understand WHY - after a structure has been given life - as God gives life to a child at birth - WHY the structure should NOT continue to manifest life!

Lack of energy is ridiculous self-imprisonment and torture!
Growing old unnecessarily is silly suicide!

Unconscious freeing of the body - frees the energy of spirit - and transforms lack of energy, lack of endurance, ill health and unnecessarily growing old - INTO all their opposites - vitality, endurance, joyous living, health, and youthfulness.

UNCONSCIOUS FREEING OF THE BODY

by

Brown Landone

CONSCIOUS MIND, 2009 YEARS TOO LATE - Lesson V

Inner muscles may not relax themselves even in sleep!
And since they can be relaxed only by NON-conscious activity,
it is wise for you to know how miraculously spirit acts with non-
conscious intelligence IN body tissues and organs.

As an example, I tell you of spirit's action in the heart.

When blood flows into the heart from the rest of the body, it
is loaded with a poison called, carbon-dioxide.
An electronic system in the heart reports the inflow, every
minute that such poison-loaded blood flows into the heart.
And that system EMPLOYS several million cells, to react to
molecules of carbon-dioxide, as an electric-eye reacts to waves of
light.

Each few MINUTES, they perform miracles, which your 'conscious
mind' could NEVER perform in more than two thousand YEARS.
This is not exaggeration.

AS blood flows into the heart, the perform seven miracles.

(1) They count every carbon-dioxide molecule of the blood;
(2) They report the numbers of molecules to nerve centers;
(3) They add the totals, as by rapid fire adding machines;
(4) They plug-in on their private telephone system, and
report the totals to motor-nerve centers in the heart;
(5) Then these same nerve centers, act as operation managers;
(6) They send messages to heart muscles to beat more rapidly;
(7) They reverse the action to slow down the heart beat, as
soon as the number of carbon-dioxide molecules in the heart is reduced so that such strenuous heart action is no longer necessary.

Conscious mind could not do even one-thousandth of this work!
Moreover, conscious mind would make thousands of mistakes.
And it could not even count one billion in 2009 years!
That would be more than 2000 years TOO late, - for unless this
work is done in four minutes, there is death to the body!

In four minutes, spirit CAN and DOES perform activities, which
'conscious mind' would take 2009 years to do!
Conscious mind is the SLOWEST AND MOST STUPID activity of soul!

-14-

It IS impossible for conscious mind even to help relaxation of inner muscles or inner organs of the body.

Even the attempt of conscious mind, causes grave consequences.

The NON-conscious freeing of the body - worked out years ago to help patients suffering from results of inner tensity - is the ONLY method I know, which DOES FREE the INNER body.

INNER relaxation - actual freedom from the tensities caused by repressed feelings - comes only by NON-conscious action.

But as soon as energies in brain centers and stopped-up energy in muscles ARE FREED, then repressed energies flow freely - restoring reactivating and even restructuring nerves and all tissues that have long been deprived of the vital life of spirit.

RESULTS of such non-conscious freeing of muscles and nerves, seem almost incredible. Real miracles of healing have been wrought by UNCONSCIOUSLY freeing the body of its inner tensities.

I stumbled on this secret of freeing inner tensity, years ago, when - as a neurologist - I found it impossible otherwise to help many pathological cases, and when I knew from my colleagues that none of them were able to do more than I was doing.

We were not then, permanently helping, 10% of such patients. But with unconscious freeing of body, there were 91% cures! Years later, I worked out the means so any one could use it - easily, simply, and enjoyably in ones home.

I repeat: Conscious mind can NOT free internal tensity! Conscious mind is the MOST STUPIDLY SLOW ACTIVITY of soul. And then also, it always HINDERS free expression of SPIRIT.

BUT SPIRIT - free of conscious mind - acts NON-consciously! Just as in the heart, it can work a thousand miracles, while slow conscious mind is merely getting ready to think about the possibility of getting ready to try to do one of them.

Conscious mind is so slow, that if you depend on it for action of the inner tissues, the action might be so delayed that it would result in death to the body.

I think you now begin to understand the bases of my previous statement that often even the attempt of conscious mind to induce relaxation of inner muscles may cause very grave consequences.

Such consequences can detrimentally affect every function of the body, - excepting only voluntary control of outer muscles.

Conscious mind can so mal-arrange distribution of blood in brain centers that insanity results; or it can so mis-function endocrine glands, that body destroys its own unified activity.

Hence nothing, perhaps, is so dangerous to the joyous functioning and spiritual response of the body, as some of the methods of
'holding thought', and some Oriental methods which teach you to
hold body activities in a non-active condition.

ALL such efforts are either direct efforts of the conscious
mind, or efforts decided upon by the conscious mind.
They always lead either to unbalanced functionings, or to
fixed thoughts and inactive conditions of internal organs.
It would take a book to present - even briefly - the ills
that can result from the "concentration effort" of conscious mind,
when you try to use it to help relax your inner body.

Relaxation can NEVER come from any conscious mind action!

The first reason is: (1) every impulse of conscious mind sent
to any part of the body to relax it, IS an impulse of activity, and
impulses of activity always tense muscles for action!

The second reason is: (2) any impulse of conscious mind sent
to stop action, does not soothingly calm it, but 'freezes' it in
fixed in-activity - crystalizing, hardening, aging the tissues.

Conscious mind always fails in trying either to activate, or
to calm and rest, any inner body activity.
In contrast, spirit works miracles of non-conscious activities -
true spiritual activities in the organs.

Vision, for instance, a portion of a large intestine - long
hollow tube - muscle-walled - skin-lined inside and out.
A surgeon takes a four foot section of such an intestinal
tube out of the body of an animal.
He keeps it in a glass tank of nutritive water for hours.
During that time, that four feet of intestine has NO connections at
all with any nerve center of the body!
It is in a small glass tank of water; not in a body.

Conscious mind can produce NO action in it.
But the spirit IN its cells can work a miracle!
If you push a small rubber ball into one end of such a
section of an intestine, it WILL squeeze the ball ALONG inside of
itself, from one end to the other.

Every day spirit works hundreds of miracles in your body.
Each and all of the endocrine glands - those master glands -
those mystic glands of mighty soul power in your body - act only
by NON-conscious and spiritually impelled power.

"What man by taking thought (conscious mind action) can add
even one cubit to his stature," - said the Christ.
But spirit is life and works miracles.
"God is spirit", and "I am the way and the LIFE".

UNCONSCIOUS FREEING OF THE BODY

by

Brown Landone

THE 6,000 BILLION LITTLE 'MOTORS' IN YOUR BODY - Lesson VI

There are 6,000,000,000,000,000 muscles-motors in your body.

So it is wise that I tell you more of the marvels of the MOTORS of your muscle cells, so that you will more fully understand, how the flow of energy in your body - and the mighty manifestations of energy in your body - are affected when inner muscles become tense and stay tense for years.

There are two kinds of muscle cells.

Some are smooth cells; some are striped cells.
One great difference is in action.
The smooth cells are very strong and work rather slowly.
The striped cells work much more rapidly.

A muscle fiber, is several muscle cells grouped together.

Each muscle fiber is a rather modest athlete.
He does not like to work naked.

Yet he does want to be free of hindrances of heavy clothing.
So he clothes himself in a thin transparent sheath - much like a pair of tights worn by an acrobat.

Since each fiber wants to work harmoniously with other muscle fibers, he oils his tights on the outside, - so there will be no friction, when they group themselves closely together for expert work.

Often these acrobats, join and work together as perfectly as a group of acrobats on a vaudeville stage.

Many of these form the larger outer muscles.
Others from all the inner muscles.
Others work alone, for the very delicate functioning of special tissues of the body.

All fibers are made up of muscle cells. There are about 6,000,000,000,000 cells in the muscles of your body.

But even a tiny muscle cell is not the smallest of the workers of these tiny yet mighty acrobats.

Each muscle fiber is made up of very delicate FIBRILS.

Please note that a fibril is only a tiny part of a fiber.

At first, the fibril may seem to be the smallest acting part of a muscle, - but even the fibril is built up of other parts.

And now lift up your heart and soul to worship the wonders of God, as you marvel at the miracle of miracles, found even in a common muscle!

Each fibril is composed of 10 boxes - white and dark boxes!
They alternate - first a white box and then a dark box.

And WHAT do you suppose these boxes are!

They are alternating electronic batteries!
A MOTOR of ten batteries in every muscle fibril unit!

Or I could designate each, as a motor of ten-cylinders!

These motors receive the spirit energy that is inspired into the body and brought to them by the nerve wires.

No matter how infinitely small they are, they are - for their size - the most powerful motors on earth!

So small that a million of these motors - each of ten batteries - could be placed inside of the hole in the letter ●, in this word one.

Yet they are so powerful, they do an immense amount of work.

And all of them work at a tremendous rate.

If playing a violin, the muscle fibers of your left hand will often make 10 movements every second, - 600 a minute!
Or if playing the 'Minute Waltz' on a piano, your right hand makes 750 movements every minute.
And the fibers of muscles of the right hand of a great pianist often makes 1260 movements in one minute!

And you and I - if speaking rapidly - require the fibers of our muscles of speech, to make 25 movements every second!
That is, 1500 times every minute!
Approximately 90,000 separate movements every hour!

It is to help you free these miracle workers from tied-up tensities, forced on them by conscious mind, - that I give you this work of Unconsciously Freeing the Body.

UNCONSCIOUS FREEING OF THE BODY

by

Brown Landone

THE LONG GRAY ROOM AND MIRACLES WROUGHT IN IT - LESSON VII

I can give you the clearest idea of just how the work of the subsequent Lessons is to be carried on, by picturing to you the room I first designed for using this method of unconsciously freeing the body to help patients.

Such a room was first arranged 57 years ago, when I was a practicing neurologist. It was fitted up to secure results which I then hoped we would get from its use.

It was a room about 30 feet wide and more than 60 feet long.

An inner wall was built to cover every window and leave only one door opening to a hall, which led to dressing rooms - one for men and one for women; and two other rooms, for a woman nurse and one for a male nurse.

Walls inside were a soft gray; and the ceiling was gray.

All lights were hidden behind frosted glass.

Then the floor of this room was covered with mattresses, which were sewed together, so that the entire floor was covered!

On top of the mattresses a soft gray carpet was laid.

There was not even one piece of furniture in the room - nothing to sit upon; and nothing to look at.

A patient suffering, sometimes for years from a nervous strain, or from inactivity of a leg or arm, or from other seemingly incurable troubles due to inner tensity or maladjustment, or from mental conditions due to feelings of frustration in life - was first taken to a dressing room.

Then clothed only in a sheet was taken from him; and the door closed. He was left alone, not disturbed for one hour.

I am certain you begin to see the significance of this:

With soft light; gray walls and ceiling; gray rug over mattressed floor; NOTHING to do except sit down on the soft mattressed floor; he was LEFT to WAIT until HE felt like doing 'something.'

The instructions given before hand, were these:

"Don't care a rap, whether you think or not.
"Just wait, until you feel some impulse to move!

"And THEN, respond to the impulse; but take no particular thought about such action, whatever it may be.

Let your body move in the way the impulse from within you impels you to move.

"The soul within you, knows more of conditions within your body, than I do. It knows how you ought to move."

The results, even from the very beginning, seemed incredible.

And still more amazing were the reports later given to me confidentially by the patients themselves - no one else ever knew anything about what a patient did or felt.

The person, for example, who had had a semi-paralyzed leg, felt like doing nothing the first three times - an hour each.

The fourth time, he began twisting his right shoulder!

He told me he twisted it in more peculiar ways than he had ever dreamed any man could move a shoulder.

Later he began to move the right side of his torso and back, twisting and turning, even rolling himself into a ball, and then straightening out again.

Each time in the room, some different action was impelled.

He never tried to think of starting any such action; but merely waited until some impulse urged him to move.

Sometimes he moved the left leg; but for weeks, there was no impulse to move the right leg which was numb and inactive.

Then the seventh week, he made a discovery - he could MOVE his right leg, much more than he had for eleven years.

Within four months, that leg had regained complete activity; and also a strength that equaled the other leg.

It is not necessary for me to give you many examples.

But this I do wish to emphasize: - I never found any two cases which worked out in exactly the same way, because of course the soul is infinite, and results of repression in each case are different from results of repression in any other case.

Another case of which I think it wise to tell you, is that of a young man of 22 years. He had suffered great disappointment in love - so serious it was almost impossible for him to sleep.

He was awake so much of each day and night that both nurses and myself began to fear for his sanity.

His first confidential report to me, after he spent the first hour in that long gray room ran something like this:

"I didn't do anything at first, but kept wishing I had a chair to sit on - squatting is uncomfortable.

"Then strangely, I began looking over my body, and realized

it was a better formed body in better condition than I had thought.

"Next I just stretched out my legs, lay back, to rest myself from the squatting which had become very uncomfortable.

"Then I stretched my arms. I do not remember just how I began stretching them, but it was strange twisting.

"Then Mr C came in and awakened me, for I had gone to sleep!"

A week later he reported, - "It's always about the same, but this time, I did not move arms and legs so aimlessly in different directions before going to sleep.

"Instead I 'discovered' I was moving muscles of my abdomen-here and there, every way - as though I were a little boy of nine, trying to find out in how many different ways I could pull the walls around - to right or left, up and down.

That's the last I remember, before I went to sleep again."

What the result would be, I did not know; but I was certain that whatever that young man would ever do in that long gray room, would be the thing which his soul knew should be done - to free the tensities of inner muscles to help draw away surplus blood from the brain centers, that forever continued thinking of his disappointment in love.

In four weeks, he was sleeping at home from twelve to fourteen hours a day; and in nine weeks he felt normal mentally and was very greatly improved physically!

Then, for a few weeks, during the quiet hour in the long gray room, he ceased moving much, but instead his mind was flooded each time with many new ideas of many different interests in life.

He remarked one day, - "It seems that as soon as I lie down and become quiet, I am a creator. So many new ideas come to me."

At the end of four months he was happy, joyous, normal again.

It was some years later, after I had studied considerably more of Truth than I had prior to that time - that I worked out the method, so any person can attain the benefit of Unconsciously Freeing the Body, by himself in his own home.

Certainly it is not necessary for you to fit up any such room as I had designed for patients.

And I have found, that it is not necessary.

It is a help, but not an essential.

I have substituted 'something else' for it, - something which I ask you to do to help to lead the mind away from definite thinking of yourself. This 'something' should be used each time before you begin to wait for impulses to morge.

I now repeat a little of what I have written, and add a little, to clarify what you are to do to free the body.

When an _outer_ muscle cramps, it prevents you from being yourself so long as it lasts. It may make you hop and yell; and while it lasts it is impossible to give your attention to anything else.

And when an INNER muscle becomes tensed and cramped, it also prevents you from being yourself - from doing anything well.

BUT since feelings of an inner muscle are NOT known to your conscious mind, you are NOT conscious of its tensed condition, although it may have continued for years.

Freeing the body _CAN_ free you of ALL such inner cramping, and work miracles because of the freed energy of spirit.

But _first_, it is NOT a system of stretching exercises.
In fact, there are NO EXERCISES of any kind.
When there is movement - stretching or whatever it may be - the full activity will come ONLY from some soul impulse, and NOT from your conscious mind.

Second, AFTER the movement has started, you will be conscious of it, but your conscious mind will NOT START it.
With no effort of thought, your soul will lead your body to do, what it most needs to do.
And you may not even be conscious of what you are doing, until after you begin doing it.

Third, vision a true idea of HOW real inner freedom FEELS.
At first, there is a consciousness of _heaviness_ in the body.
With true relaxation, there is _never_ a feeling of lightness - for when the body relaxes, it wants to slump down and rest.

Fourth, you may find it strange, that at first - perhaps for days - there will be MORE fatigue than usual.
IF _SO_, _GOOD_. It means your inner muscles _are_ letting go.
Since they are no longer trying to 'keep going', the new tiredness is not a fatigue of exhaustion, but the fatigue of REST cells no longer pretending, but truly letting go to rest.

If _such fatigue_ comes to you, bless _it_. Do not worry.
_It_ _is_ soul rest for your nerves. And as soon as they are rested in this way, the body will respond amazingly to its impulses.

Fifth, realize that YOUR soul _IS_ infinite, and that it is enfolded _IN_ God's infinite LOVE.

This suggests what your attitude should be, in this work.
Always feel that God's love is enfolding you, inspiring you, impelling you - to use the particular movement which YOU need to use, to free your inner body, to let spirit act freely.

UNCONSCIOUS FREEING OF THE BODY

by

Brown Landone

THE NEED OF MORE EXPRESSION OF SPIRIT - Lesson VIII

For every LACK in HEALTH, one needs to express more of the soul's energy through the parts of the body which need healing.

For more ABUNDANCE, one needs greater consciousness of power - in handling conditions and other people.

For more STRENGTH, one needs greater bodily freedom in letting the soul's energy express through the body.

For COMPANIONSHIP - or mateship - one needs more adaptable responsiveness in joyously and continuously manifesting more of spirit to others.

For JOY OF LIFE, one needs spiritual impulsiveness, manifesting constantly and unlimitedly through the body.

FOR UNITY with God and the highest spiritual attainment, one needs the true spiritual responsiveness of the body, so that one can receive illumination by spirit, and readily respond to it.

FOR ALL of the above there is need not only of responsiveness of body, but of brain centers also!
If brain is not responsive enough to spirit, then there is lack of thought, lack of feeling, lack of high ideals, lack of in-spiration, lack of consciousness of peace and love and joy and power.

Study and often restudy the next four sentences:

"In SPIRIT, my body is the holy temple of my soul.

"In INDIVIDUALITY, my body is the instrument of my soul, - for it is by USE of parts of my body, that I can produce words, tones, and actions. And they are the only means which can make me likeable to others; the only means by which I can express my love to others; the only means by which I can express power in establish-ing and maintaining myself with others."

"In ACTION, my body is the motor my soul uses."

"In YOUTHFULNESS, my body is the radiance of my soul. More than bones and flesh; it is living spirit in expression!"

AND ATTAINMENT of all the above desired conditions, is blocked by ALL TENSED conditions of inner muscles, which tend to prevent all expressions of soul energy.

Our purpose is to free the tensity, for greater expression!

To follow directions of succeeding Lessons effectively, first learn the difference between direct thinking and imagining.

Direct thought tenses the body; but imaging frees it!

Thinking about doing anything turns energy toward the muscles you would use in the doing, and this tenses muscles.

Direct thought directs thought TO yourself!

But "imaging" - as I teach it to you in these Lessons - leads OUT TO ideals beyond the self!

Hence it prevents your throught from being directed toward your inner self.

Imaging is the first step, leading OUT to ideals beyond the self. It FREES inner muscles instead of tensing them.

Begin by imaging the immensity of your soul, to begin to relieve internal tensity, to release blocked-up conditions, and to free limitless energy.

Have you ever thought of the SIZE of your SOUL?

You have heard it said, that "the soul is infinite."

You believe it; but when you try to 'think' it, it is difficult, even though you repeat the thought many times.

So now try IMAGING the immensity of your soul.

First look at your body. It may be 14 to 20 inches across the shoulders; it may be 5 feet to 6 feet tall!

And for years you have been trying to find your infinite soul 'inside' that little body! It does not make sense!

Infinity can not be crowded into such a little body!

So what is the truth of the relationship of soul and body?

Your body is only the focal point of your soul!

It is the point from which your soul extends infinitely out from your body, and far beyond your body.

A stove is the focal point of the heat of the fire in it.

The heat is the spirit of the fire.

It radiates far out beyond the stove.

The heat fills the entire room!

The stove is only the focal point from which it radiates.

So also your body is but the little focal point, from which your soul, as spiritual power, radiates out beyond the body.

IMAGE another picture of the limitlessness of your soul!
Your soul is the radiating activity of spirit!
It is made like unto the activity of God!
Image God as the infinite spiritual activity of the universe,
always radiating out from his focal point of existence.

ALL higher energies radiate - shine out from a center.
There is NO energy of the universe that does not radiate.

God is radiant spirit, - like sunshine of the sun.
The sun is only a focal point of the sunshine.
The sunshine fills all space 93 million miles out to earth;
143 millions of miles to Mars; 482 millions of miles to Jupiter,
and all space millions of millions times farther beyond earth and
Mars and Jupiter.
The SUNSHINE you feel IS the SOUL of the sun.
It is not enclosed within the sun; it exists beyond the sun.

So also your soul is not enclosed within your body.
Your body is but the focal point of your soul's radiation.

Image it in another way; image your soul as the radiance
of a spiritual broadcasting station.
Whatever is broadcast is NEVER INSIDE the station itself.
Its electronic waves radiate for thousands of miles in all
directions, so that music broadcast from a station in New York, can
be heard in London or Rio Janiero or Delhi or Cairo, as well as in
every home in our own land.

Your soul is spiritual radiance; never confined in your body!

Spend two minutes each night and morning, imaging your body as
the physical focal point, from which YOU - as spiritual power - are
radiating out beyond that little body.

Spend another two minutes each night and morning, realizing your
soul IS spiritual radiation - infinitely surrounding your body and
penetrating to every cell, but never 'enclosed' within so little a
thing as a body!

Take this FIRST step, to lead your thought away from your
body, so that you will no longer cause spiritual stagnation within
the body, because of conscious mind's effort to make you believe
that your infinite soul is squeezed and packed inside a little body.

Freedom of concept of soul, leads to freedom within the body.

Begin as above to prepare, for freedom in expressing soul.

UNCONSCIOUS FREEING OF THE BODY

by

Brown Landone

THE VISION BEFORE THE ACTION - LESSON IX

The second step is to begin to <u>unite</u> the ideal of your body <u>with</u> your ideal of your infinite soul ever FLOWING OUT from God.

What now follows will take the place of the Long Gray Room! <u>This is the VISION OF CHANGE - from frozen ice to growing life!</u>

<u>Vision two great hillsides</u>, a valley between, and a river blocked up by caked chunks of ICE and masses of frozen SNOW.

Vision the infinite POWER of the SUN - and its increasing warmth with the coming of spring.
<u>Vision the warm sunshine MELTING the ice and snow.</u>

Vision the POWER of sunbeams, <u>freeing</u> locked-up masses!
Vision the power GRAVITY "pulling" water down stream!

Vision the water - destroying nothing - yet washing out and carrying away all clogged and dammed-up ice and snow - becoming <u>a river of majestic power, flowing freely to its destiny.</u>

Night and morning, repeat this visioning of winter and hillsides of snow; frozen ice of a river; the coming of spring; warmth of the sun; melting of the ice; the free flowing river!
Vision this so many times, that you can think it at any time!

Then, vision dams of snowed-in-thoughts and frozen-feelings!
And divine love around you, melting and washing out all ice.
The river of life flowing down between beautiful woodland and fields, grass and flowers growing with new life; the soul of earth awakening and expressing itself!

Vision this also, until it becomes so habitual that you can recall it on an instant.

Use these visions whenever you begin any of the work that follows in subsequent Lessons.

Think often: "In my body, there is no hindering tensity - no blocked-up feeling, no frozen thought - that can not be melted by the warmth of the love of God, and the joy of my own soul.
The POWERFUL FLOW of my soul - flowing in a STREAM OF LIFE out from God - is awakening to new life, freeing it to grow anew, to manifest freely, to fulfill its destiny."

UNCONSCIOUS FREEING OF THE BODY

by

Brown Landone

UNDERSTANDING RELAXATION AND DIVINE INDIFFERENCE - LESSON X

Freeing the Body is the Soul's natural process:
(1) of laying thought quietly aside,
(2) of releasing the tensity of inner muscles,
(3) of freeing the body to respond,
(4) to the soul's impulses to move freely.

We know four truths of the effects of direct thinking:
(1) MENTAL strain tenses muscles greatly;
(2) ALL effortful thinking tends to TENSE muscles;
(3) ALL direct thinking IS effort of the mind;
(4) Direct thinking turns thoughts to the soul's self.

Hence you can NOT relax by thinking you are going to relax!
Such effort is a contradiction in itself, - for EVERY thought does
tense one muscle or another - every mind-reader knows that - and
you cannot relax from tensity of thought by more tensity of thought.

When you think of relaxing, you may induce the large outer
muscles to let go for a while, BUT you tense the inner muscles!

The second step to freedom was given in the preceding Lesson.

The third step is to learn DIVINE INDIFFERENCE.
If you feel, - "I don't care a rap whether I relax or not,"
you at once free yourself of the EFFORT of TRYING to RELAX!
And then the body can really begin to relax.

There is also a difference (1) between "adjustment" done by
others FOR you, and (2) adjustment from within, BY your own soul.
When organs or bones are displaced by accidents or strain,
they should be adjusted by others or by conscious exercise.

But 99% of all mal-adjustments are caused by tensity of inner
muscles, which pull inner tissues out of place.
And NO ONE CAN free your tensed inner muscles for you.

SOUL KNOWS WHICH inner muscles are tensed. With Unconscious
Freeing of the Body, the soul frees them, so each misplaced organ
or tissue adjusts itself normally and keeps itself in place.

By day, look to the sky - by night look to the stars - to
realize - "My soul is infinite; I do not care a rap whether or not
I try to free my body! Soul is free; LET IT free my body!"

UNCONSCIOUS FREEING OF THE BODY

by

Brown Landone

VISION THINKING THAT DOES NOT PRODUCE TENSITY - Lesson XI

I have already led you to realize the limitless extension of the immensity of your soul, surrounding and permeating your body.

In that Lesson, I asked you NOT to 'think' of that immensity, but to image its immensity - to picture it as infinite spirit radiating from your body as a focal center, - just as electronic waves radiate for thousands of miles out beyond a broadcasting station which is nothing but the focal point of the radiation.

Yet now I ask you to THINK, but to think in a VISIONING WAY.
Vital vivid thought is picture thinking - imaging something OUTSIDE the self - that is, in terms of something else.

Such thinking takes thought away from the self - frees self.

Think of your soul, as a soul beam shining out from God - so radiant that it can NOT be shut up inside your little 2 by 6 body any more than a rainbow can be shut up in an ink bottle.

Think without letting your conscious mind tie you down to limited fixed thoughts, for they always tend to create a subconscious conflict within the soul.
Your soul wishes to express its infinity.
Your conscious mind is always trying to cork it up
And hence, its efforts create conflicts within you.

Think CLEARLY: "My body is very small, my soul is infinite".

Think DEFINITELY: "My body is only the focal point of my soul's expression; merely the point from which I manifest in life".

Think HONESTLY: "Since I know that my soul IS infinite, I know that it surrounds my body as well as acts through it."

Think VIVIDLY: "My soul is a stream from God.
It IS an actual stream - continuously flowing out - radiated by God - infinite power - capable of meeting every need."

All problems - business, personal, health - are first worked out in the soul; then the body acts, to EXPRESS the result.

Reread this Lesson once a day, for at least seven days - as the third step in preparing to Unconsciously Free Your Body!

UNCONSCIOUS FREEING OF THE BODY

by

Brown Landone

THE PREPARATORY PREPARATION - LESSON XII

Relaxation is a RESULT!
You can NOT free the body BY relaxation.

Instead you free it FOR relaxation - to attain the result
of freedom of body for greater freedom of the soul in action!

The following is the initial view of preparatory preparation!

FIRST, choose a time - PREFERABLY at night - or early morning
when you can be ALONE in your own room for this work.

SECOND, remove restricting clothing, and arrange bed clothes
so that they will not hinder your movement or even suggest that
you are tucked in or held down by them.

THIRD, lie down for quiet rest and close your eyes; vision
your own soul as sunlight surrounding and penetrating your body.

FOURTH, vision again two great hillsides of life!
Vision the infinite sun power of your own soul melting all
obstructions and letting life flow freely through YOUR body!

FIFTH, then WAIT!

SIXTH, IF and WHEN an impulse comes to move, - then move!
Do NOT think of what you OUGHT to do or ought NOT to do!
When you feel like moving, do so.

I do NOT "advise" stretching or any other activity!
I advise ONLY that you WAIT, and follow the impulse!

If it is an impulse to move, then move - for such an impulse
is a divine voice of your soul indicating the particular movement
necessary to release the dammed up energy in your body.
    If there is vigorous movement, do not stop it, SO LONG as
the movement comes from an IMPULSE to move.

SEVENTH, IF you feel NO impulse to action, be content and
bless God - for soul is resting inner nerves.

Spiritual impulse is THE test! It is the result of God-Wisdom.
What you or what I think, is tinged with lack of conscious understanding. But the impulse of spirit is divine direction.

UNCONSCIOUS FREEING OF THE BODY

by

Brown Landone

INITIATE THE FREEING ACTION - LESSON XIII

The preceding Lesson gave the vision of the work of this one.
This Lesson tells of action to fulfill the vision.

Begin now the actual Unconscious Freeing of your Body, to free
each and ALL tensities of all inner muscles, to free all unbalanced
blood flow, to free all nerves of all conditions that hinder the
free flow of soul's energy THROUGH your body and OUT OF your
body into joyously free expression!

Carry on the work as given in this Lesson for two weeks -
each night for the two weeks!
OR each morning if you prefer, - although in life, as lived
today - it is wiser to do it, at night before you go to sleep.
And also before your prayer for unity with the Infinite.

For this work, it IS necessary to have a room by yourself,
while freeing the body; and always better to use a wide bed.
Nevertheless, do not worry if your bed is a narrow bed, - for
after all, the real work is done from deep within your soul.

When you have things arranged for the night, so there is nothing more for you to attend to, - then - when quite undressed - lie
on your bed without any intention of making any definite movement,
and also without intending not to do so.

First vision the change from the frozen ice to the flowing
river of life.
Vision that vision first! It, in itself, may be enough to
start the freeing process, - for it leads all conscious thought
away from yourself to the images you vision.

The actual step is willingness, unconsciously to respond in
action, to any awakening subconscious impulse to move.

Feel as free as possible - soul, mind, body - free!
Then just WAIT - ready to feel any impulse awakening in you,
and willing to move any part of the body in any way.
And above all, when an impulse comes, do NOT try to direct
any responding movement by conscious mind.
Let conscious mind recognize it, but NOT direct it.

LET FREE ACTIVITY follow, EVERY impulse TO MOVE!
Roll, twist, stretch - ANY movement you feel like doing!

Any part of the body, or all of it!

If excessive activity is what your body needs, the outer muscles WILL be VERY ACTIVE - you may pull your body this way or that, roll up into a ball; twist your neck as though trying to pull it from your body; put your head between your knees; et cetera.

Continue responding to any impulse that comes, until you feel within you, that you want to stop and pray and go to sleep.
And IF there is NO impulse at all - that also is good - for it means, that in your condition, inactivity is best for the time.

Your soul knows what your body most needs, so the first few nights may be times of quiet.
BUT LET action come, if there is an impulse to move!

You CAN tell when a movement comes from impulse, because at such a time, something within you seems to make you move.
If action is due to your conscious mind, it will follow some idea, such as - I THINK I'LL do this or that.
But impelling desire is from the soul! You will move FIRST, and then AFTERWARDS recognize that you are moving.

And how long should you continue this?
Continue this phase of the work each night for two weeks,
Then follow suggestions given in the next Lesson.

And how long should you continue the work which follows?
Perhaps for a month! Perhaps a year!
Continue UNTIL you ARE free!
Until all ill conditions ARE remedied!

Continue, until your soul expression is so free and powerful that it changes your body and frees your soul, so that you are healthy, so that organs are vital, inactive parts active again.
Continue until YOU are capable of handling every personal or business problem you are called upon to handle.

Then every morning, give a few moments, to idealizing the IMMENSITY of your soul - infinitely greater than your body.
Imagine your soul so infinite, that you can look on spiritually, and seemingly observe the attitudes of your body and the actions of your body without feeling bound to them.

This should NOT result in a sense of detachment from your body!
Instead, it should be consciousness of the immensity of your soul enfolding and permeating your body - consciousness that your soul is so much greater than the body through which it manifests, that YOU - the soul - are free to use any power of your soul, to note what the body is doing and even enjoy what it is doing!

UNCONSCIOUS FREEING OF THE BODY

by

Brown Landone

GREATER 'SPACE' FOR FREER MOVEMENT - LESSON XIV

After your first two weeks of Freeing your Body on your bed, seek a larger space, for your subconscious mind may hold back some impulses to move, unless it knows that there is amply space for more extended and freer movement.

For the extended freedom of space, move furniture back near the walls to give the largest possible free floor space!

Spread a blanket or quilt or comforter on the floor.
Remove most of your clothing.
And lie on the floor for a few minutes.

Vision again the visioning given in Lesson IX.
Then wait for some unconscious impulse to move.

Then stretch or pull or twist your body - just as you did when on the bed; but never unless you FEEL like doing so.

AFTER 10 or 15 minutes, if you feel drowsy, go to bed!
OR, if you receive a "spiritual hunch" of how to solve a certain problem, go to bed to let your soul complete the plan for you unconsciously and without effort, while you sleep.
OR, if you feel an inflow of energy, to do some work that needs to be done, do it - but only if it is convenient to do it, and will not disturb others in the home!

Often when I feel tired, I lie down, intending to sleep.
BUT, after a few minutes of Unconsciously Freeing my Body, such inflow of energy comes, that I get up; do hours of good work.

Most fatigue is not due to need of sleep! It is not due to any wear and tear on the body.
Most of our desire for sleep is due to inner tensity or to the monotony of work we have been doing.

Whatever you do, after the impulsively initiated movements on the floor, will be best for you!
If your nerves need rest, you will feel MOTIONLESS and drowsy.
If it has this effect, Free the Body BEFORE you go to bed.
If your nerves need awakening, you will feel inflow of energy.
If it has this effect in YOUR case, then perhaps, it will be wise to change the time of Freeing the Body, and do it in the morning so that you can use the newly awakened energy during the day..

CAUTION: KEEP WARM! If weather is cold, or room cool, or
floor drafty - do NOT use the floor - but continue work in bed.

Sometimes - when Freeing the Body - you will feel impelled to
act ridiculously. Yet this may be divine wisdom.
What is ridiculous for adult, is often joyously normal for child.
And if impulsive energy has been IMPRISONED deep within you
since childhood, and is now striving to express itself, let it FREE
itself; even though the movements seem ridiculous.

Note what I did one day when I was a child. I was an invalid
in a wheel chair during most of my first seventeen years of life.
I was able to walk a little, only now and then.
One day, when seven, I put my little fist through one window
pane after another, and they were small panes difficult to smash.

Adults said I was destructive; I could NOT understand myself.
But NOW I know what impelled that action.
In my condition, breaking a window pane was neither right nor
wrong in itself. My soul was longing for action.
Others were wrong to repress my energy, by keeping me in bed.
Such an OUTBURST of energy in breaking window panes, was just
what was needed at that time, to make me KNOW that I DID have
strength, when doctors and nurses kept insisting I did not have
enough energy to get well - that is, that there was no hope of my
living more than a few months.

That action of my childhood was due to continuously repressed
activity. Doctors, nurses, everybody - kept me from DOING anything.
— They were sincere; afraid I'd tire myself, make myself worse.
But IF anyone at that time had known of the method I know now
of Unconsciously Freeing the Body, all my repressed energy could
have been expressed - easily, joyously and freely; and it is
probable that I would have become well ten years before I did.

Ten years later at seventeen, I was still not expected to live
three months - the same verdict, every month since childhood.
And to help you realize more fully the miracles that are
wrought when repressed energy is freed, I think I should tell you more.

It was only when I experienced emotional explosion against
an injustice, that I awakened enough energy to get into such
activity, that as a result, I was well within a year.

FREEDOM OF THE SOUL in expression is the ONLY means by which
life of spirit can COME INTO ACTION - freeing the body, restructuring it, reactivating it, giving new life and new joy in living and
new power in attainment.

UNCONSCIOUS FREEING OF THE BODY

by

Brown Landone

TRUST SPIRIT, - IF NO ACTION, IT IS GOOD - LESSON XV

For a time, there MAY be NO need of activity of the outer muscles, and hence no such activity in YOUR case.

Hence for many nights, you MAY lie quiet -- with NO action of external muscles at all!

If this happens, then MOTIONLESS quiet is what YOU need!

Follow the subconscious impulse - whatever it is!
If for movement, move; if for quiet, lie MOTIONLESS!

Trust spirit in you - it knows every little tensed muscle or your inner body; it knows just what inner or outer action, just what feeling, will most quickly and completely free you.

Soul knows every congestion of blood due to any inner tensity, and what is best to free the tensity causing it.

It knows just what portions of your body, what organs of your body are thrilled with energy so they are overactive, or deprived of energy so that they are weakened.

And it will impel you to do exactly what should be done for the best and quickest results FOR YOU.

No impulse to move will come, unless it should be followed -- for the soul id DIVINE and KNOWS what is NEEDED!

As you continue the work, soul and body become ONE, and your divine power comes into actual manifestation.

Do not be concerned if - after one period of action - there follows a period of NO impulse to make any movement at all.
There are periods - sometimes lasting a few hours, sometimes days, sometimes for weeks - during which the nerves - like trees in winter time - need complete rest for inner growth.

If you have been impelled to make certain movements for a day or a week, and then they cease for a time, it is evident that the previous movements have freed certain inner muscles enough to give their nerves a time for a winter of inner GROWTH!

When MORE movement is NEEDED, it WILL come!
Since you do not consciously know what action is needed, keep up the work each day - knowing that movement or NO-movement is beneficial, for the SOUL KNOWS when each is needed.

UNCONSCIOUS FREEING OF THE BODY

by

Brown Landone

THE SPIRITUAL ATTITUDE OF LIFE - LESSON XVI

CONTINUE Freeing your Body - for the more the body is freed of inner tensity, the more the soul manifests, fully and freely.

I myself have used this Unconscious Freeing of the Body for three generations. I shall continue to use it (just as I shall continue to breathe air) as long as I have a body.

RESPOND to soul impulses! In Freeing the Body, each impulse comes from the Spirit, and the physical movements are naught but responses to that complete consciousness of the soul that KNOWS what each part of the body should do to free conditions within.

The important thing is RESPONSE to the impulses of spirit!

Respond and you will marvel at the results in yourself, - for freeing the body, for free flow of divine energy, gives the freedom necessary for the soul to do the particular thing needed to be done, and the inspiration of how to do it!

This is more than relaxation - a thousand times more!

It is the SPIRITUAL FREEDOM of soul, manifesting spirit!

From the greater freer flow of spirit in the body - comes all the results of greater expression of energy and spirit!

First comes the feeling of becoming free; then the freeing of fixed ideas of the mind, or the freeing of stiffened muscles; then awakening of new activity; the revival of vitality in every organ of the body; a new restructuring of the tissues - in fact a new youthfulness!

When more spirit flows through body transformation takes place.

Then other freedoms follow - freedom from all the repressions of the past - a new life, with new freedom of joy, and responsiveness to joy such as you have never known before.

The more you free yourself from the consciousness of separation, the more you manifest the spirit of God in unity and PURITY.

I write this, because sometimes, when Freeing the Body, a new feeling of sex is awakened to consciousness and vitality!

IF it comes in your case, 't will come:

(1) because all cells of your body need the life and vitality of divine sex energy all through your body, to rejuvenate it;

Or (2) because you lack assertive power in dealing with others;

Or (3) because you lack creative ability in handling things or conceiving new ideas or ideals;

Or (4) because you need to stop condemning sex, and need to be spiritually awakened so that you will idealize it, as the divine impulse of life from God.

Idealize it, instead of condemning it.
When you condemn anything of the soul, you separate it from God (in your consciousness); and thus you create a dual world of conflict within yourself, instead of soul harmony unified with God.

It IS good - for it IS life - the CREATIVE power of GOD.
Since God is all there is, all that he created is good.

Hence if this new awakening comes, idealize it and accept it as the particular power you need most at this time, to reawaken new means of new life for you - to create your body ANEW.

Then OFTEN, another awakening comes - perhaps quite unexpectedly - a tremendous new consciousness of love, that reaches out to others as it has never reached out before in your life.
It may be love not only for those near you, and for those whom you know, but also an expanding love, like the love of Christ.

It may seem strange, and yet when it awakens, you will know that it has always been deep within your infinite soul.
And that - with the body freeing itself - and more of the soul expressing itself - more of the love of the soul also comes into expression.

Then too, YOU may experience another kind of awakening - a true SPIRITUAL ILLUMINATION of spiritual feeling within.

And communication also - not a mere message in words, but something greater and grander - the feeling that you are actually in spirit, completely enfolded in spirit - communing spirit to spirit with all great souls of all ages of the past - informed by them, guided by them, protected by them!
Accept such communion of the saints of spirit.
And greatest will be the awakening of communion with God.

BODY PURIFICATION

By
Brown Landone

LESSON I - PURIFY, OR DIE

Commit to memory, these self-evident Truths:

(1) Spirituality is the manifestation of the Spirit of God in Man.

(2) If man is not manifesting the Spirit of God, he is not spiritual.

(3) Manifest means "to make plain, or to make evident, or to make obvious."

(4) Obvious means, "So evident that you cannot help but see it."

(5) Spirituality is manifestation, so evident you cannot help but see it.

Yet you see fine old church deacons, so crippled with rheumatism that it is very evident that their spirituality is NOT MANIFESTING in their bodies.

You have seen sweet souled preachers - so soggy and loose muscled or dried up and shrunken that it is obvious that Spirit is not manifesting in their bodies.

You have seen divinely unselfish leaders of Truth grow fat - so fat, that it is quite evident that Spirit has not yet manifested in their bodies.

You have seen thousands, consecratedly thinking spiritual thoughts, yet needing 7 hours sleep, and dying even before they are 80 years of age.

Judge not; but praise God for the idealism each such soul has attained.

Then grow in your own idea of spirituality, so that you can help yourself and aid others to be spiritual of body as well as of mind. Add to your previous ideal of spirituality; make it greater, grander, and not so limited. For unless your body is pure in the true sense, spirituality - with all its power, its blessings, its health, its vitality and the actual riches it brings - will not be yours.

Certainly one must be pure in thought and pure in living to be pure in body. Such purity is necessary. But it is not all that is necessary to attain a pure body.

I bring you a new ideal of purity - one of complete unity - pure thinking and pure living, in a pure body. Just as you have seen a clean bodied person in dirty greasy overalls, so also you have seen many a pure soul, in a body saturated with fatigue, poisons, loaded with waste mineral matter, bloated with poisons of food fermentation.

That is why I stress purity of body as well as purity of mind.

What is 'pure' and what is 'purity?' What do we mean by a pure body?

Gold is pure, if not mixed with tin or nickel or anything not natural to it.

Milk is pure, when not mixed with any substance not natural to milk.

A thing or substance is pure when not mixed with anything unnatural to it.

And the same principle determines purity of thought and love.

When one speaks of pure love, we mean love which is not mixed up with any attitude or feeling which does not exist in the nature of love itself.

It is the only true ideal of purity, and so a human body is pure when it contains no substance not a part of the true nature of the tissues of the body.

Purity of mind depends on ideals. Purity of body on purity of substance.

But purity is not limited to one substance. Pure milk contains many substances - water, cream fat, sugar, proteins, mineral substances, and vitamins. These in the right proportion form pure milk. It is pure when it contains (1) only the substances natural to itself and (2) contains them in the right proportions.

Hence, a pure body is one which contains (1) no waste substances not natural to it, and (2) only the right proportion of substances of which it should be composed - for an over-amount of a normal substance makes a body impure.

Bile, for instance, is a fluid precious to your body. Yet if there is twice as much bile as there should be in your body, the extra amount becomes a deadly poison.

It poisons the blood and entire structure of the body so that it is almost impossible for you to drag yourself around. It even produces poisons in the brain cells and gives you a sick headache. It poisons the nerves, until you are so weakened that your legs wabble.

Purification of the body is the process of ridding the body of every waste not natural to it, so that nothing shall hinder the free flow of soul energy.

But why bother to purify the body?

Well, what is the difference between the stiffened,painful and rheumatic muscles of an old man, and the supple muscles of youth? What is the difference between hardened arteries and high blood pressure of middle age, and the elastic blood tubes and buoyant heart beat of youth? What is the difference between the burdened body - so loaded with lime salt wastes - so loaded that the soul's energy can scarcely get through it, and the youthful body - so responsive, that God's energy manifesting through it, makes it feel so joyous that it wishes to play all day and dance all night?

There is but one basic difference.

When the bodily tissues are loaded with waste materials, there is lack of suppleness, lack of buoyancy, lack of energy, lack of strength, lack of youthfulness - for your mind-energy cannot plow through such wastes without using up much of its power.

But when the bodily tissues are purified - when they are free of wastes - then the limitless energy of your soul is eager to manifest in joyous movement.

Ill health is nothing but lodgement of waste material in the body. Fatigue is nothing but piling up poisons which should be removed. Slowed-down brain action and painful nerves are nothing but poisoned nerve cells. Old age is nothing but hardened arteries and stiffened muscles, loaded with waste lime-salts.

Physiologists themselves know that there is no cause for disease or weariness or even growing old, except lodgement of waste materials and poisons in the body.

Listen to the evidences:
"Were it not for the liver, which destroys many poisons, and the kidneys, bowels and skin, which eliminate poisons, we would speedily die.
"In fact, as it is, we almost always do die of poisons.
"The only real exception is when we are killed by physical violence.
"Poison, therefore, is the main factor in causing old age and death not directly due to injury.
"Carrel has kept the heart tissue of a chicken alive in the laboratory by periodically washing out the poisons produced by its own life processes. Repeatedly it became senile, and about to die, but was at once rejuvenated by a thorough washing out.

"It will be seen, therefore, how extremely important it is to reduce our daily dose of poisons." (1)

And another: "Old age is decrepitude --- the spine is not so supple, the cartilage disks between vertebrae shrink. The spine collapses and 'stoops with age'. The knees are bent, the hip joints stiff. The muscles shrink." (2)

Remember (2) that the word 'toxic' means poisonous; (b) that anything that is hardened or stiffened is loaded with mineral wastes; and (c) that hardening of the arteries is inevitably the cause of growing old. Then recognize the importance of the following:

"In youth the arteries are elastic, but as the body grows old, they become stiffer on account of the replacement of their elastic tissue by fibrous tissues and lime salts.
"In many cases the arteries - - - may be markedly thickened and even so calcified as to have earned the term Goose-neck arteries - because the deposit of lime salts gives them a corrugated feeling like that of a goose as one feels its neck.
"In myocardial (heart muscle) degeneration - - - the same symptoms occur. The most frequent causes of myocardial disease are (1) the deposit of scar-tissues around sclerotic or hardened arteries and capillaries.
"'Rheumatism' deserves a special word - - - it includes some twenty or thirty separate diseases, ranging from rheumatic fever - - to the chronic progressive, deforming arthritis about which we know very little save that it continues remorselessly until nearly all the joints are chalky, twisted, and rigid.
"The commonest form of deafness is a chronic sclerosis or hardening of all the tissues, drum and ossicles, of the middle ear.
"Dizziness is just as much an indication of vestibular disease as blindness is an indication of disease of the eye, or deafness of the ear - - - it may be temporary, due to a toxic cause." (3)

And there are many other poisons left as waste in the body - the waste products of dead bodies of cells for instance. One spoonful of blood contains about thirty billion red blood cells. Yet within ten days, new living cells will have taken their place, and those 30,000,000,000 little living beings will all be dead bodies broken up as waste material by the liver, and all this waste should be eliminated.

But this is only the ten day waste of one spoonful of blood. Think then of the dead waste of the billions and billions of other cells of all the organs. No wonder we grow sick and diseased when the body is not daily purified of such dead material.

(1) "How to Live", p 65, by E. L. Fish, M.D. Hygiene Reference Board, Life Extension Institute.
(2) "Why We Behave Like Human Beings", p 37, by George A. Dorsey, Ph.D., Ll.D., Formerly Associate Professor Anthropology University of Chicago.
(3) "The Human Body", pp 161, 149, 66, 244, 250 - by Logan Clendening, M.D.

Not only hardened arteries, but what is called the "Hard" liver, and stones in the kidneys or bladder are due to great over amounts of lime salts, and other wastes.

Stone in the kidneys or bladder is a very common condition. We now know that most nervous diseases are due to conditions outside of the nerves. "Probably the most important single results that has been reached in our study of nervous diseases in the last 15 years, is the realization that the cause of them in easily 80% of all cases lies entirely outside of the nervous system - - - The man or woman who is nervous has poisoned nerve cells - - - direct saturation of the tissues with toxic substances." (4)

Dr. Carrel has kept tissue cells of the heart alive for 16 years, after the chicken from which the tissue was taken, had died.

In writing of this Dr. Fisk says, "These cells are multiplying and growing, apparently unchanged by time - to all appearances immortal so long as they are periodically washed of poison and nourished."

Where then shall you begin? Why with your mind of course.

Just as your body is not pure if it contains a wrong substance. so your mind is not pure if it contains a wrong idea. You have not realized that each thing produces after its own kind. Pure thinking, purifies the thought; pure ethical living purifies the character; but pure physical living is necessary to purify the body - each in accord with God's Law after its own kind.

Even though you have modeled your ethical life in accord with Christ, you do need to use soap and water to clean your hands when they are dirty. Soap and water, accomplishing their end after their kind, are just as divine as pure thought accomplishing its end after its kind.

So purify your mind of the wrong idea that pure thought can be substituted for pure bodily living. Such an idea is not spiritual - God never taught that you could substitute a pine tree for an apple tree or vice versa. God's law is each thing after its own kind - pure bodily living is essential to a pure body.

In this Course, I teach you how to purify the body:
FIRST: of wastes and fatigue poisons produced within the body; how they are results of activity; why they are so poisonous that the body must give way to a stupor-sleep to get rid of them; how they may have accumulated for years so that there is now continued exhaustion; how to prevent production of such a large amount daily; and how to get rid of those which do result from necessary work.
SECOND: of the mineral wastes which are being taken into the body daily, and which have been taken into the body, and are now deposited in the body; what foods or drinks carry such wastes into the body; why they are not carried out; how they may be dissolved within the body; how they may be forced from the tissues into the blood so that they will be eliminated.

(4) Woods Hutchinson, M.D.

-5-

THIRD: Of the cutting and grinding acid crystals - the results of abnormal fermentation and souring of foods or lack of proper functioning in the body.

FOURTH: Of the physiological wastes - those wastes which are just as normal as ashes in a grate but which clog up energy if not removed.

FIFTH: Of the serious disintegrative poisons due to disintegration of cells which have lived their length of life; why they are such deadly poisons - as deadly as the materials of a decaying body; how they poison organs so that diseases originate; how they furnish breeding soil for germs; why it is just as impossible for soul energy to manifest through these as it is for life to manifest in a dead body; and how to free the body of them.

SIXTH: Of the emotive poisons - wastes produced by negative emotions or by lack of joyous and mirthful emotions; why they can produce tremendous results even in a few minutes; to what extent ones body is still poisoned by emotions of years ago; why some people seem to find it impossible to be joyous or mirthful; how to neutralize these wastes; how to get rid of those long existing in the body; and how to eliminate those produced day by day, so that the body shall become responsive to the energy of the soul.

What can you do about it? - - - Why, about anything you please.

I shall give you proofs of what has been done as well as methods.
Mineral lime salts deposited and hardened int the body are the most difficult to remove. Yet, even this has been done. I cite a case which was considered hopeless - deposits of lime in the walls of the heart. For seventeen years, no specialist examined the person, except to declare that he could not live more than three months from the time of the examination. Yet he is still alive, healthy, vital.

Another man at eighty years of age was so stiff, rheumatic, and tissues so hardened he could scarcely move. Yet, at ninety, he was a physical culture trainer.

Dr. Carrel has astounded scientists. He has taken tissues from dead bodies and kept them living - such as heart tissue of a chicken dead a generation ago.

Scientists now agree that the one thing which causes disease -. old age, and death are waste poisons not removed. When removed, cells have almost immortal life.

What then, may you not do with your body?

By

Brown Landone

LESSON II - THE NEGLECT WHICH COSTS YOU ONE-SIXTH OF YOUR LIFE

Whether or not you purify your body is not a matter of "life" and "death", but it is a matter of life or death.

One scientist has said that - unless killed by accident - "WE DIE BY INCHES". (1) That is, we begin dying years before we pass on.

Science has lately proved there is NO reason for growing old, except that we neglect to keep the body purified of wastes taken into it or produced by it.

Fatigue poisons are one of the most destructive wastes.
Fatigue poisons act differently with different individuals.

Accumulating in one body, fatigue wastes may so poison the structure that nature will demand a lot of extra water to thin and weaken the poisons so that they will not actually kill the cells of the body. In such a case the person becomes fat.

Of course, such fat is not oil fat. But then, very few people ever become stout from oil fat. Most of the fat is water bloat, due either to fermentation of food or to extra water the blood needs to dilute and weaken the poisons left between cells. This saves the body from death for the time, but it does make one fat.

Being water bloat fat, no amount of dieting can permanently reduce such fat.

Nothing but purification of the body will accomplish the result desired.

In another person, fatigue poisons may settle in internal organs - digestive organs, liver, pancreas, et cetera - so that those organs are so poisoned that they do not fulfill their functions completely. Hence, such people become exceedingly thin.

In one person, fatigue poisons will poison nerve and brain cells, until the cells scream with pain, urging the individual to get rid of the poison.

In another, fatigue poisons may deaden nerve and brain cells, so that nerve paths are exhausted and paralyzed and brain cells numb and dazed.

Fatigue wastes result from use of bodily tissues and are always poisonous.

They are produced (a) by any and every activity of nerve or brain cells; (b) by every movement of any muscle, whether used in work or play; (c) by all work done by cells found in the bodily fluids - blood, lymph, et cetera; and (d) by all the physiological work of any and every organ or gland of the body.

(1) "Why We Behave Like Human Beings", p 252 - by G. A. Dorsey, Ph.D., Ll.D.

Whenever a muscle is moved, mind energy works through millions of cells in that muscle. And even before that muscle moves, the mind energy works through brain centers and nerve paths, using more millions of cells.

Whenever a cell works, part of its structure is broken down as waste material. If this is not carried away, it lodges as fatigue poison between cells.

It is difficult to realize the immensity of work done by the body. Your body is a universe of cells and you are the god of it. The number of cells cannot be conceived by a human mind. On earth there are 1,700,000,000 people, but in your body there are more than 25,000,000,000,000,000 cells. Every cell is a little living individual. Your mine, your love, your spirit animates every cell of your body.

All of these individuals work - they do an immense amount of work every minute.

Swelling peas cooked in a pot will lift a cover held down with a 160 pound weight; and cells of a growing tree will lift tons of matter hundreds of feet above the ground. Yet our bodily cells exert more energy than any other kind of cell in the universe.

Just to balance our head on our spine with every step we take, we use 144 muscles; and with every step we put more than 100,000,000 little individuals to work.

Then there are the cells of all the organs which keep up their work night and day from even before we are born until after we have passed on.

"The work done by both ventricles of the heart in 24 hours has been calculated by a conservative physiologist at 14,000 kilogrammetres - this is sufficient work to raise a man of 150 pounds twice the height of the Woolworth Tower." (2)

It takes thousands of cells to make one little neuron of a brain cell - and yet, when a snow ball hits you, that impact sets about 10,000,000,000 neurons to work.

Whenever any cell of the 25,000,000,000,000,000 cells of the body works, it throws off fatigue wastes. So unless the body is continuously purified, it soon becomes loaded with poisons. Then the nerves are numbed or shriek with pain; brain cells scream out protests at being poisoned; muscles play out or cramp; the heart becomes so fatigued it misses beats; and each organ is so drugged it fails to function properly.

(2) "The Human Body", by Logan Glendening, M.D. p 141.

If you continue work, without constantly getting rid of the fatigue wastes, fatigue poisons accumulate and the cells are completely surrounded and perhaps saturated with the poisons; muscles are poisoned to such a degree that soul energy cannot manifest through them even if it reaches them from the brain centers; brain cells become so poisoned and exhausted that they become numb; and great accumulation of fatigue poisons so saturates the structure of the brain centers that mind cannot even act through the brain. Then one sinks into a stupor-sleep so that no more wastes shall be produced until the poisons already in the body are partly eliminated.

It may seem strange that there are poisonous substances through which mind itself can not pass. Yet, it is in accord with God's law. The only reason it may seem strange to you is that you have mis-interpreted the statement that "mind is everything".

When a mental scientist says 'Mind is everything,' he means that mind is the source of everything. That is true. God made each thing, each after a law of its own. He made light so that its rays can pass through glass yet can not pass through concrete walls. He made sound to pass through miles of air, yet unable to pass through a bale of cotton. He made mind so that it can manifest through a pure body, yet not pass through certain poisons. This is infinite wisdom. If it were not so, fatigue poisons would accumulate without any elimination and thus poison the body unto death.

Your mind manifests easily through pure bodily substances, but - in accord with God's plan - it will not manifest through poisonous material. Prove this for yourself; stand before a mirror; extend your right arm out from the shoulder and hold it in front of you on a level with your shoulder. Then bend your first finger in toward the palm as far as you can; now straighten it out as far as you can. Continue this for fifteen minutes, if you can. Then decide if there does not come a time when you can not move your finger, or even hold up your arm.

There are poisons through which the mind can not act. Fatigue poison is one of them. A man of great will may be able to hold out for many days' continuous work, but finally the mind refuses to continue the effort because the accumulation of fatigue poisons prevents soul activity from acting through the muscles.
Every time a person sleeps, he proves that there are substances through which mind does not act. The only reason he sleeps is because his mind cannot easily manifest through the fatigue poisons which he allows to over-accumulate while awake.

Laziness means that the body has not been active enough in eliminating fatigue poisons. Some people are always tired; even their brain centers are so tired that they do not even desire to arouse themselves to activity. As soon as the tissues are cleared of fatigue poisons, such an individual wants to be active. The first step is hard muscle work to press waste poisons into the blood so that they can be eliminated. It is oftentimes difficult to help lazy people overcome their laziness because they do not want to take the first step. They usually want you to do something for them, before they do the hard muscle work. Their salvation lies within themselves.

As soon as fatigue poisons are eliminated from the body, the body is ready for work and ready for play - for it is only when there is an abnormal amount of fatigue poisons in the body or some lack of nerve connection between the brain centers and the muscles, that one feels habitually lazy or continuously tired.

No soul is lazy. Laziness is a bodily condition - a body soggy and poisoned to such a degree that the life force will not manifest through it easily.

The fatigue poisons of the body are produced at all times, even during sleep, but during sleep they are quite completely eliminated, if the sleep is normal.

There are THREE means of purifying the body of fatigue wastes.
First, by emotions which produce chemicals which neutralize fatigue poisons.
Second, by increased elimination by means of the skin and kidneys.
Third, by elimination of fatigue poisons by the Breath of Purification.

The use of emotions in neutralizing fatigue poisons is so important that I do not discuss it here; I give an entire lesson to it. Elimination of many wastes by the skin and kidneys is so important that three other lessons are given to it.

Probably you have thought that lungs and breathing have but one purpose.
That is a mistake. Each organ has two or three functions.
Breathing has many functions: (1) in general it supplies oxygen and helps to regulate temperature of the body; (2) functioning certain lobes of the lungs awakens definite brain centers; functioning in another way deadens them; portional breathing can increase activity of the endocrine glands - the ductless glands - adrenals, generative glands, pineal gland, pituitary gland, et cetera.

And the kind of breath taught in this Lesson is the Purification Breath.
It helps to eliminate the fatigue poisons brought to the lungs by the blood. It is the Breath of Purification. It will help to change you from a life of fatigue and lack of energy to one of constant purification and vitalized power.

Of course, ultimately you should make the Breath of Purification a habit, so that every few minutes, without even thinking about it, you will use it.

The Breath of Purification should be taken as follows:
Sit erect but not tense; or stand easily on both feet.
(1) Take air into the lungs, while you quickly count FOUR.
(2) Slowly relax, letting air out of lungs, while you slowly count SEVEN.
(3) Repeat each inhalation and each exhalation, thirteen times.

Remember, breathing can be used for many purposes. You can breathe so that you actually help to keep fatigue poisons in your body. Or, you can breathe - using this Breath of Purification - so that quantities of fatigue poisons are rapidly carried out of the body. For this, everything depends on the counts, and the rate of counting.

By making the outgoing breath longer in time than the incoming breath, greater time is given for the transmission of the fatigue poisons from the blood in the walls of lungs to the air in the lungs. Hence, the purification of the body.

Always count four for the intaking breath quickly. Always count seven for the outgoing breath slowly. Always repeat these thirteen times at each use.
This numbering is not fantastic. Science has proved that such inhalation and exhalation remove twice as much poison as is removed by ordinary breathing. This breath rate should not be used all the time - for breathing has other functions. It should be used only for purification - when fatigued, or to prevent fatigue.

First, use it merely as a matter of purification to relieve you of fatigue. Then let it grow into a habit, so that whenever you begin to be fatigued, you will begin to use the Breath of Purification without even knowing it.

Remember, Quick counting of four for the ingoing breath; the slow counting of seven for the outgoing breath; and the repetition of the breath thirteen times.
You can repeat these thirteen breaths as many times each day as you need.

Here is another aid I give in this lesson. It is not a matter of purification but it helps to increase energy when it is most needed.

You know that runners used to carry 'corncobs' in their hands while running races. Now at sporting goods stores, they buy little rubber or wooden rolls, which they grip while running. There is a reason for this. It keeps up endurance, and postpones fatigue by keeping energy in the body.

Many a woman spending a day shopping - instead of letting her hands hang loose and becoming tired - has found abundant energy by closing her hands while walking from one store to another.

You know also that whenever you desire to hold determinedly to a decision - you set your jaw. That also has a purpose - to keep energy within the brain centers.

In over-coming fatigue, purify the body of waste poisons and also hold the energy in the body because you most need it when you are fatigued.

So, when using this Breath of Purification, firmly close your jaws, and firmly close each hand into a fist. Keep all the body relaxed, except the jaws and hands.

(I sometimes hesitate to give this aid because some people overdo it. There should be NO tension anywhere, except in the jaws and the hands. Then it is very energizing.)

BODY PURIFICATION

BY
Brown Landone

LESSON III - THE SAVIOR OF THE HUMAN BODY

One kind of water hardens your arteries, tends to produce a
'solid' liver, forms 'stones' in the kidneys and gall bladder, and
brings you to an early grave.

Another kind of water dissolves the very mineral wastes which
produce the condition just named, washing them out of your body and
making you young again.

So, certainly, the subject of water is puzzling as well as important.

Be certian of this: I shall never urge you to drink more water
than you want.
I shall not suggest that you take 4 or 40 glassfuls of water a
day to drink.

It is not necessary to 'take' water as drinking water, unless
you want it.
You can obtain quarts of water in delicious foods and drinks
made with water.

Your body can be purified without drinking a gallon a day, as
faddists advise.

For myself, I cannot remember when I have taken a whole glassful
of water as drinking water. Yet, old as I am, I have kept my body so
cleansed for more than twenty-five years, that I have been able to work
and play from 20 to 22 hours each day.

I do not under-estimate the value of water in the body.
For the processes of life, water is the most important of all
substances.

The amount of water in the body astounds one - two thirds of your
body is water. If you now weigh 175 pounds, and were dried out, you
would weigh only 55 pounds.
"Bones are nearly half water - - - and half the entire water content
of the body is found in muscles." (1)
Even the so-called solid organs, liver and kidneys, are just as
watery as a potato, which may not mean much until you realize that a
small half pound potato contains almost a tumblerful of water. Potato
is nearly all water.
"Muscles, liver and kidney hold as much water in proportion to
their weight as does the potato - - - and even bone - - - is more than
one-third water." (2)

(1) "Why We Behave Like Human Beings," by G. A. Dorsey, Ph.D., LLD.
(2) "Foundations of Nutrition" by M. S. Rose, Ph.D., Professor of
    Nutrition, Columbia University.

"Cells depend upon having their food transported to them by the water route (the blood) - which requires about ten pounds of water constantly in circulation." (3)

"The cells also depend upon having their waste products flushed away, so there must be waste-bearing water (urine) while there is life." (4)

Blood and lymph form the transporting system of the body.
"Over 90% of the blood of our transport system is water." (5)
"Brain tissue is 85% water." (6)

"Water is the great dissolvent of food before it is taken into the cells." (7)

"The water excretion of our body carries off in solution countless organic substances, as well as chlorides, bromides, iodides, phosphates, potassium, sodium, ammonia, magnesium, iron, carbon dioxide, nitrogen, argon, et cetera." (8)

"First on life's bill of fare is water. No water, no life." (9)

"Without water, no living process takes place.
"Nothing can take its place for washing away all body's sins." (10)

Taking water into the body and then excreting it by lungs, skin and kidneys, is the one way of keeping man from burning his body to death.
If it were not for this use of water in lowering of temperature, the heat from the intake of food would burn up the body within a few days.
Water is the one great essential - as a solvent, as food transport, as a flushing system, and as a heat regulator. No digestive process, no eliminative process, no heart action, no breathing, no life process, can take place without water.

What is water, and yet - - - -!

Since one kind of water takes most of the mineral matter into the body and leaves its mineral deposits there; and since another kind dissolves those mineral deposits and washes them out of the body, it is important to decide what kind of water to use in purifying the body - to change it from a stiffened and hardened old body, to a body supple, buoyant and youthful with energy.

At least eight kinds of water are advocated for health purposes by one faddist or another - hard water and soft water; raw water and boiled water; rain water and snow water; filtered water and distilled water.

Hard water is water which is saturated with lime salts and other minerals. In leaving mineral deposits in the body, it is most harmful.

_____

(3-4) "Foundations of Nutrition" by M. S. Rose, Ph.D.
(5-10 incl) "Why We Behave Like Human Beings" by G. A Dorsey, PhD. LLD.

All kinds of water usually used for cooking and drinking - that is, all kinds of water from all kinds of private or public water systems - are hard waters.

Some are harder than others - but all such waters are hard - for any water, which has run through or over ground, is hard water.

Naturally many city water systems - which take water from rivers and lakes, or reservoirs supplied with mountain water - call their supply soft water. But soft water from such sources is soft only in comparison with water which is harder.

All such soft waters contain great quantities of mineral matter. Even the water running in rivers to the sea, contains an enormous amount of mineral matter.

"Each year the earth's rivers carry to the sea five billion tons of dissolved minerals and other unnumbered millions of tons of carbon compounds." (11)

There are also the hard waters which are called mineral waters - that is, waters from certain mineral springs - well known for their medicinal effect. Practically all kinds of 'bottled' waters are hard waters.

Some people are helped by drinking waters of mineral springs, for such waters often help to cleanse the liver, the kidneys, and the intestines. Hence, for those who need such waters, the benefits of using such mineral waters - if used for a short time only - greatly over-balance any detrimental deposits of mineral matter left in the tissues of the body during the short time such waters are used.

But the use of any ordinary water - any water generally used - leaves a very considerable amount of hardening material in the bones and softer tissues.

Raw water is water which has not been boiled. Raw water may be hard or soft - as hard as lime water or as soft as rain water. It may contain millions of germs, with every drop densely inhabited. The most dangerous germs are the typhoid germs.

Boiled water is advised by some health authorities. Boiling removes none of the lime material, although it does kill some of the germs in most raw water. But the dead bodies of these germs are carried into the system when the boiled water is used. Such dead material furnishes a fertilized soil for rapid and lusty propagation of germs already in the body. By drinking boiled water one may avoid live disease germs but he takes into his body the best dead germ soil for the growth of other germs.

(11) "Why We Behave Like Human Beings"- by G. A. Dorsey.

While raw water is an aquarium, boiled water is a graveyard.

Rain water is water which has been distilled by the heat of the sun. When distilled (up in the clouds) it contains no mineral matter and no germs.

But, when it falls from the clouds as rain, it falls through air filled with germs, dust, smoke, and dirt. By the time it reaches the earth as rain water, it is so saturated with decaying matter and with dirt that its color is yellowish.

If rain water is allowed to stand it becomes filthy because of rotting animal matter in it. I discuss it only because some 'nature' faddists are so ignorant that they advise the use of rain water on the basis that it is 'natural'.

Snow water is melted snow. Snow is frozen rain. The freezing does not destroy many germs. Snow looks white and clean, but it contains germs and dirt just as rain water does. Remember the dirt left from melting snow in the spring - how the dirt of what has melted forms on top of the snow which is not yet melted.

Filtered water is water which has passed through a very fine strainer called a 'filter'. The use of filtered water was once popular. People supposed that water which had passed through a filter was purified. They believed that the filter kept the waste substances and disease germs of the water in the filter. While it is true that some lime and other solid substances are kept in the filter by filtering, yet, there is no filter made which can prevent germs passing through its fine meshes. Each pore of the finest filter is large enough for a hundred germs to march through side by side in gleeful company with head and tails up.

Moreover, decaying matter collects on the bottom of every filter. This forms an excellent breeding ground for germs. Hence, after a filter has been used for a few days, the filtered water often contains more disease germs than the water which is put into the filter. Germs are grown by the millions in the collected wastes at the base of the filter, and washed through with the filtered water.

Distilled water is water which has been turned into steam, so that all its impurities are left behind. Then it is turned back into pure water. It is the only water which is pure; the only water free from all impurities.

When you distill water saturated with blue ink, the distilled water comes from the distill, pure and crystal clear - with every impurity removed.

Distilling water turns it into steam and then back again into water. Steam can not carry a particle of mineral matter; it will not carry disease germs, dead or alive, or any waste product of any kind.

If pure distilled water is boiled in a teakettle, NO lime will collect to coat the inside of the kettle even though you use the same kettle for ten years.

Distilled water is the only pure water on earth.

Yet, some faddists and health teachers object to distilled water on the ground that its life has been taken out of it. This is silly ignorance. The only life in any water is the life of the germs in the water. We should not drink water to get life from germs. The divine purpose of water is to regulate temperature and to act as a solvent.

In nature, water in evaporation is so fine that your eye cannot perceive it, as it is drawn up into clouds. Then it falls as rain so that it can again evaporate and cool the surface of the earth, keeping it from being parched and burned.

As a solvent, it dissolves rocks and soil and carries their substances into the sap of the plant.

In the human body, water fulfills the same two functions: it regulates the temperature of the body by helping to get rid of the extra heat resulting from some 3000 calories of food taken each day. Water saves the body from burning up.

And it also acts as a solvent in the body. It dissolves food substances so that they can be assimilated and taken to every cell of the body; it dissolves the wastes of cell life so that those poisons can be carried away from the cells. It dissolves mineral substances lodged in tissues of the body so that such substances can be eliminated in the process of purifying the body.

Distilled water is the greatest solvent on earth; the only one that can be taken into the body without damage to the tissues.

By its continued use, it is possible to dissolve mineral substances, acid crystals, and all the other waste products of the body without injuring the tissues.

For purification, distilled water is the solvent to be used. After wastes are dissolved, muscular exercise can force the dissolved poisons and wastes from the tissues into the blood, so that the blood can carry such wastes to the excretory organs. Then, those organs can squeeze and pour the wastes out of the body.

Remember that great scientists now not only admit but assert that all old age, and even death - unless by accident - is due to waste poisons not washed out of the body (12), that Dr. Carrel has made heart tissue "apparently immortal by regularly washing away the wastes of the cells (13), that distilled water is the great solvent, and that "nothing can take its place in washing away our body's sins." (14).

(12-13) - Dr. Eugene L. Fisk, M.D.
(14) - Logan Glendening, M.D.

BODY PURIFICATION

By
Brown Landone

LESSON IV

BREAK DOWN THE "GREAT WALLS OF CHINA" WHICH EXIST IN YOUR BODY

Purification removes wastes, and brings the body to a perfect balance.

If it is too fat, it becomes thinner; if too thin, it becomes normal.
The basic cause of modern fatness is accumulation of waste materials lodged in the tissues, and betweenthe cells which blocks up the flow of energy and demands that other substances be deposited to neutralize the waste. That produces fatness.
The cause of undue thinness is poisoning of internal organs by wastes, so that they do not properly digest food eaten, so that it can build up the body.

One great purpose of purification is bodily balance.
The other is great increase of normal energy.

Few people realize that they build stone walls around the bodily cells, so that the cells are imprisoned. It's NO exaggeration to call them stone walls.

A new teakettle is so clean on the inside that it shines. Yet, after boiling water in it for one week only, a lime coating of stone forms on the inside.

The reason is this: when you boil water, a little evaporates and leaves the mineral matter behind as a deposit. The more water boiled, the more lime left. After a few weeks' use, the inside of a teakettle is thickly coated with lime deposits.

And water evaporates even when it is not hot enough to boil.
The sun shines on a little pond back of my home. Of course, its water never boils, yet there is heat enough of the sunshine to evaporate four feet of water from all over the top of that pond even during a cold summer. Its level would sink four feet, if extra water were not supplied by springs.

Even when water is merely warmed, it evaporates and leaves lime deposits.
Now consider evaporation in the human body. You eat food enough to produce 3,000 calories every day. At least your body daily produces some 2500 units of heat energy - enough to raise your temperature 150 degrees each 24 hours.

Two thirds of your body is water. You take a half gallon or more water - in food and drink - each day. This water, by drainage and evaporation, continually reduces the temperature of the body and keeps its heat down to normal. If this heat were not carried off by water, your body would burn up within a few days.

But even at normal bodily temperature, water evaporates, so that mineral deposits are left - unless the body is purified and the wastes washed out.

Even in one week's time, the water boiled in a teakettle leaves a stone coating of lime. You take at least one half gallon of water, sometimes a gallon, every day - as drinking water, or water in which foods are cooked, or water used in tea, coffee, et cetera.

Remember also that cities' so-called 'soft-water' from reservoirs supplied by lakes or rivers, is also loaded with minerals. The soft water rivers of earth carry 5,000,000,000 tons of mineral to the sea every twelve months.

Think what happens to the inside of a tea kettle in one week; realize what happens to the inside of your body in thirty years.

How much lime do you think will collect in your body by the time you are thirty years old? That's why the body grows older, stiffer and harder each year.

Stone walls are really the cause of the difference between youth and age. The movements of the child are responsive. Its hopping and skipping is done lightly and airily. How can it run and jump and play so easily?

In youth - before the body is loaded with waste deposits - each cell receives enough soul energy from brain centers to give it sufficient force to uphold itself.

Watch a little child hop, skip, and jump. When merely playing it will skip and hop one third the height of its body and do so for hours a day.

Yet, even if you at 20 years of age tried to jump and skip as high in proportion to your height, you would be exhausted in ten minutes. So much waste has accumulated in the body even at 20 years, that the body cannot uphold itself easily. It is loaded with wastes in proportion to its weight, so that joy of movement is gone.

And in old age, every cell may be so loaded that it is almost impossible to move with ease and still more impossible to move with the joy and buoyancy of youth.

But the most impure body - the body most laden with wastes - can be cleaned. It can be purified. I am not stating a theory. I refer to what has been done.

I shall cite actual cases in the next Lesson - in one case it has been done even after the man was 80 years old.

But at this point, remember these two self-evident facts:

(a) when cells are not encumbered by mineral waste matter, they easily and readily respond to the energy which comes to them from the mind.

(b) when cells are encased in limestone shells in later life, and also separated from one another by the walls of poisonous waste matter, the energy which reaches nerve cells and muscles is so reduced that there is little kept for action - only just enough to cause motion, with NO surplus for buoyancy, no joy in movement, and no youthfulness.

Many times I have distilled ten gallons of water such as is furnished in large cities by public water systems. Always there was left more than one-fifth of a glassful of lime mud. Even though you drink little water, you take 10 gallons in one way or another at least every 12 days, and a full glassful of lime mud every 60 days.

It is no wonder our arteries harden, and produce high blood pressure; no wonder we grow old; no wonder we lose the suppleness of youth. No wonder we tire easily. No wonder elimination processes are hindered and we grow fat.

Extra mineral matter lodges in the cartileginous endings at the joints and hardens and stiffens them so that movement becomes painful. Hardened cartileginous ends may rub against each other - cutting and grinding one hardened tissue against another.

Mineral waste may also lodge in muscles, causing them to become stiffened and sore. We often mistake this condition for real rheumatism. In this hardened and stiffened condition, it is impossible for nerve energy to flow through them easily. When it makes the attempt there is pain, because of the effort to break down the hindering substances; and there is also fatigue; and lack of endurance because so much energy is used up in plowing its way through the obstructing waste materials.

But there is never any lack in mind - never any lack of soul energy.

It is only the impurities lodged IN the body which hinders soul manifestation. It is only when bodily tissues are impure, that limitless energy cannot flow freely through them, just as sunshine cannot shine in fullness through a smoky glass.

Mineral deposits build up stone walls, and it is a- difficult for energy to get through them as it was for old Asiatics to break through the great wall of China.

Differences in energy and vitality - illness vs health, dragginess vs buoyancy, weakness vs endurance, laziness and fatigue vs joy in action, and wrinkled age vs renewed youth - are illustrated by Chart One and Chart Two.

Chart ONE represents tissues of an impure body, loaded with wastes.

"BC" represents the soul's brain-center dynamo of a loaded body;
"NP" represents the nerve paths of such an impure body;
"L" represents losses of energy used up in breaking through wastes;
"O" represents the organs of such a waste-filled body;
"M" represents its muscles, saturated with acid crystals and
lime wastes;
"E" is each 1000 units of soul energy, trying to manifest in such
a body.

The bodily tissues illustrated in this Chart are impure - poisoned
by fatigue wastes; stiffened by acid crystals from wastes of food, loaded
with mineral matter, so that it is almost impossible for each 1000 units
of soul energy to plow its way through the wastes - whether along nerve
paths, in organs, or in and through muscles.

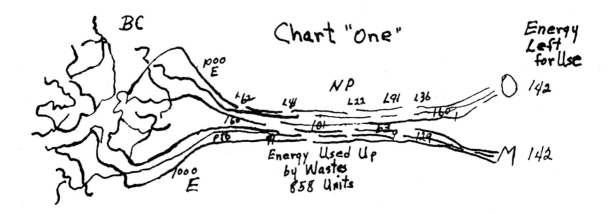

By the time each 1000 units of energy has plowed its way to the
organs or muscles of such an impure body, 858 units have been used up.

Hence, there are only 142 units left for use.

Now on the next page, learn what energy you can have for use, if
you wish - for a purified body does not limit or hinder the soul's
manifestation. God created man spiritually and physically - to manifest
His power.

This is Chart Two representing tissues of a purified body, responsive to mind. Of each 1000 units of soul energy, note how much is left for use.

"BC" represents the same physical dynamo; "NP" the same Nerve Paths; "O" the organs of the body; "M" the muscles; and "E" the 1000 units of power.

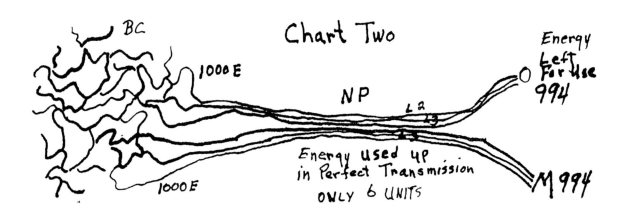

In such a purified body, the tissues ARE responsive.

Hence, each 1000 unit power, radiated by mind - from physical dynamo - loses only 6 units of energy by time it manifests in and through organs and muscles.

Losing only 6 units out of every 1000 units of power, leaves 994 for use.

This gives an abundance supply of energy to the organs and to the muscles, (a) to keep organs at healthy work, and (b) to give muscles buoyant power.

What is the difference? Out of every 1000 units of soul energy, a purified body has 7 times as much energy to use, as has the impure body. That is why some individuals have abounding energy, while others have scarcely enough to drag around.

There is never any lack of soul energy.

Every lack of energy felt by the body is due to the impurities lodged within the body itself. Every bodily impurity offers resistance to the energy of the soul.

In the next Lesson- what Has been done, and How to do it.

By
Brown Landone

LESSON V - HOW TO DISSOLVE AND REMOVE MINERAL WASTES
WHICH FIRST LOAD DOWN TISSUES AND THEN HARDEN THEM.

You know about water - at least you know about eight kinds of it, and you know that the water which you use, and nearly everyone uses, hardens your arteries.

You also know that hardened arteries are the basic cause of growing old. Yet the worst case known to medical science of a hardened and stiffened body was remedied. It was a case of purifying the body of mineral deposits - the case of the late Captain Goddard Diamond of San Francisco. The result secured was astounding in that the hardening of arteries had affected his entire body. And inasmuch as he did not begin to remedy the condition until after he was 79 years old, it is even more astounding.

Captain Diamond was born in 1796, and was 80 years old in 1876.

At that time, it was difficult for him to move. His legs and back were so stiffened he could not rise from a chair or sit down without help. His arms were so stiff and his fingers so twisted that it was difficult to hold a knife and fork to feed himself. In his condition it took nearly nine years to purify his body, but he did it.

At 90, he was teaching a class in physical culture. At 108, he daily road a bicycle; and in 1904, he was the oldest physical culture instructor in the world.

He did purify his body of the mineral deposits which had accumulated during eighty years. How he did it, I shall tell you in this lesson.

And here is another case - actual solidification of inside walls of the heart.

Physicians could not understand the thumping action of my father's heart during his last years, nor why he should have such difficulty in breathing.

They knew nothing of the cause of his trouble; the only thing they did know was that my heart was acting just as my father's acted. My father died in April, and the physicians - all of them specialists - told me I could not live till June.

I felt that my one hope was knowledge - to find out what had been the trouble with my father's heart, so that I would know what to do for myself.

It was before the time of X-Ray so we determined to have a post mortem examination. It revealed that the inner walls of my father's heart had become actually saturated and hardened with lime to a depth of from 1/32 to 1/8 of an inch. This mineral waste was not outside of the tissues of the heart, but actually in the muscular tissues. At the base of the valves it was 1.8 of an inch deep. This was caused by the lime which the muscle cells had taken from the blood passing through the heart.

As the valves could not work properly, the heart had been forced to make a desperate and continued effort for years to keep the blood in circulation. This had stretched the heart so that it was nearly as large as a beef heart. It was this increase in size which had caused the difficulty in breathing.

I was then seventeen and from every indication, I had exactly the same trouble, and had had it for years. In fact, I was born an invalid and no physician, when he examined me, ever gave me more than three months to live. Yet, I did live on.

After the post-mortem examination of my father's heart, I realized that there was but one thing for me to do - wash the lime deposits out of my body. In order to live, I had to purify my physical heart, and all the rest of my body.

For two years, I purified my body of mineral wastes, until my heart seemed to be in good condition. Then I waited four years. When I was 24, I had examinations made by the specialists who had previously declared that my heart trouble was incurable.

When the re-examination was made, they found no trace of either organic or functional heart trouble. Of course, they could not believe the evidence of their own examination. So although they did admit that they then found no trace of the heart trouble, each one of them was certain that it would return later.

Then years more passed - very busy ones - and then at 34, I was again examined by heart specialists, who found NO trace of heart trouble.

More years passed. In 1925, I was again examined by a great heart specialist who used all the marvelous means now available. Heart beats were photographed. With fluoroscopy, specialists actually looked into my heart. They found it perfectly formed; and pronounced it sound, functionally and organically.

So I know that for two generations, I have had no trace of heart trouble.

What I did to help dissolve and eliminate the lime-accumulated in the muscles of my heart was heroic. It was not as wisely done as I could do it today, with what I now know of purification, but it did work the results.

For two years, I lived on fresh watery-non-acid fruits, leaf products, a very few cereals, a little red meat, and quantities of distilled water. I nearly died on that diet, but it did clean my body.

Captain Diamond lived on about the same diet, except that he took approximately a quarter glass of olive oil each day, and devised certain muscular exercises which helped to squeeze the lime out of the muscles into the blood, after it had been dissolved by the distilled water which he used.

(I do not recommend Captain Diamond's use of olive oil for purification purposes, but his exercises - given at the close of this Lesson - ARE very effective. Olive oil was helpful to Captain Diamond because he was old, very thin, and needed to build up flesh and provide extra heat for his body.)

Of course, you have no such condition as Captain Diamond and myself had to remedy, but your body is being loaded up with lime wastes and mineral substances.

Certainly, man needs a certain amount of calcium, phosphorous, and iron every day of his life. Even though the bones have completed their growth, they must continue to grow the red cells of the blood which are produced in the red marrow of the bones. These necessary amounts of mineral matter do not total more than 2½ grams. A gram is a very small part of an ounce. Yet, you take into the body a fifth or a sixth of a glassful of lime wastes in the water you use every twelve to fourteen days. Such lime is mostly waste; it does not contain the salts needed by the body.

Only a very small amount of real mineral substance is needed for normal growth and health, and such substances should be obtained from foods, not from the mud lime found in drinking-water. Since so little is needed, imagine what happens to your body when one-fifth of a glass of mud lime is taken in drinking water every 12 days.

You know the results: When mineral matter lodges in the walls of the arteries, they become hardened so that their walls begin to lose their power of contracting and expanding. Even with a little hardening they are not able to force blood through the body without great tear and strain on the heart, and consequently high blood pressure.

When the over-amount of mineral lodges in bone tissues, they become harder and more brittle. Muscles attached to the bones are stiffened at the joints. In the bones, less red blood cells are produced and this hinders elimination of other wastes.

These wastes lodge in nerve tissues and in between cells and thus prevent mind energy from radiating from one brain center to another.
If the waste matter happens to be deposited in the sight centers of the brain or along the optic nerve we have failing vision and perhaps blindness.
If it is deposited in the hearing centers of the brain or in the nerves which run to the ear, we may have deafness or partial deafness.
It may even disconnect nerve centers, stopping the nerve current. producing complete isolation of ideas. This results in the condition which we call "second childhood".

What are you going to do about it, and how?

You may bathe your body three times a day so that your body is unusually clean, yet, that does not clean the greasy overalls in which your body does its work.

You may think pure thoughts, and live a clean pure life - yet that does not purify the body in which your mind does its work.

In my Studio windows, I have the purest window glass made for transmission of all rays of light. It transmits all visible colors and also ultra-violet rays.

But last night, stormy weather blew smoke from the fireplace; and today, the panes are dirty with soot and smoke. Sunlight is the all powerful energy of light, yet smoke on the panes does hinder it from shining into my Study.

What shall I do? Shall I use Truth as a Christian Scientist, declaring that the smoke is an illusion of error, and that it does NOT exist on my window panes?

Or, shall I use Truth as a Diving Scientist, declaring that light is being, and that smoke is 'not being' and that not being cannot hinder being.

Or, shall I use affirmation - asserting that sunlight is the all powerful light, and that smoke has NO power to prevent it from shining in fullness into my Study?

Or, shall I use Truth as a Mental Scientist - sitting with my eyes closed - declaring that the all power of mind will make the soot vanish from the window pane?

Or, shall I use Truth as an absolutist and refuse to use any material means (such as arm motion), to clean those window panes?

Or, shall I use the Great Truth - which includes wisdom and all God created?

I do not depend on material means when I take a cloth to clean window panes.

When I take a cloth instead of a thought to clean smoke from window panes, I depend on God's wisdom which tells me to use "each thing after its own kind."

All powerful sunlight is hindered by the smoky dirt on window panes the expression of your soul is hindered by the dirt in your body. So, what will you do?

First, choose your food wisely; (a) avoid those dry foods which carry unnecessary amounts of mineral substances into the body; and (b) eat freely of watery foods.

Here is a list of watery foods; the water content of lean beef is 80%; potatoes 84%; apples 85%; oranges 87%; cabbage 92%; carrots 88%; string beans 94%; tomatoes 95%; lettuce 98%; and each of these foods is also very rich in mineral salts and vitamins.

Eat foods which contain the largest proportion of water to mineral elements; carrots have a water content of 8,860% of the mineral content; in whole wheat bread the percentage of water to mineral is 3,800%; in beef, 7,400%; in spinach, 4,635%.

And here is a list of the dryest foods: The water content of
almonds is 4.8%; of pine nuts 3.4%; of pecans 3.2%; English walnuts
2.8%; peanuts only 2.5%.

The water content of peanuts is only 72% of their mineral content,
while the water content of spinach is 4,635% of its mineral content;
and spinach contains more mineral salts than peanuts contain. Nuts are
the dryest foods.

(The coconut is an exception. The heavy protein of peanuts is
531% of that of coconuts; while the water of coconuts is 783% of that
of peanuts.)

Nuts leave much mineral waste in the body, because they do not
contain enough water to help wash out their own wastes in the body.
Moreover, being so dry, they use up water from the body and tend to
dry up the blood. The use of nuts by our pioneer fathers helped to
age them while young in years. A man of fifty was then often stiff
in the joints, bent of back, and aged.

The body needs water, "Even bone - - - is more than one third
water." (1)

So eat quantities of the foods which contain the largest quantities
of water. Use the list of "watery foods" to judge other foods. In
water content, beets are much like carrots; chard, spinach and celery
much like lettuce.

Choose foods which will wash out the waste materials from the body
- for the water of all fresh vegetables and fruits is distilled water,
and acts as a solvent.

Even a half pound potato contains nearly a tumblerful of water.

The second step in eliminating salts is the use of distilled water.
Since water is so essential to every process of life, use distilled
water which meets every need and also dissolves the lime salts. For
this, nothing equals distilled water.

Use distilled water (a) for making your coffee and tea, (b) for
all baking, and (c) use nothing but distilled water as 'drinking water'.
(But do not cook fresh vegetables in distilled water. It dissolves their
salts and you lose them.)

Distilled water in bottles can be purchased at drug stores or
grocery stores.

Third: Use tensing exercises and force waste materials out of
the large muscles into the blood so that they can be eliminated after
being dissolved by distilled water.

_____

(1) "Foundations of Nutrition" by M. S. Rose, Ph.D.

Tensing exercise ONE: (a) stand easily on both feet, with all of the body relaxed; (b) extend arms at sides on a level with shoulders; (c) partially close the fingers as though gripping an orange; (d) then grip as though trying to crush an imaginary orange in both hands; (e) hold this tensity while you count seven; and then relax.

Use this three times a day - morning, noon, and night.

Tensing exercise TWO: (a) stand easily with all of the body relaxed; (b) gradually bend knees; (c) slowly sink to an easy squatting position; (d) next, plan to push the floor away from you; (e) then tense the leg muscles as though pushing the whole earth away from you; (f) make the tensed muscles push your body up to a standing position; (g) repeat three times slowly.

Use this exercise three times a day, immediately after exercise one.

Youthfulness is of the Spirit, and manifestation of Spirit is spirituality.

You are not spiritual if you are fat. You are not spiritual if you are thin.

You are not spiritual if you are continually tired, or if you are growing old. You are not spiritual if your body is so loaded with fatigue poisons that you sleep 7 hours a day to get rid of the drunken stupor due to such poisons.

If you are vital, mirthful, supplied with riches, and growing younger, then you are spiritual - for these ARE evidences of God in manifestation.

BODY PURIFICATION

By
BROWN LANDONE

LESSON VI - IT IS BLOAT WHICH MAKES PEOPLE STOUT AND FAT

For thirty years I have declared again and again that fat foods, of themselves, will not and cannot make a person fat.

Sometimes a few facts contain more truth than a dozen 'scientific' theories.

First, NO restricted diet will permanently reduce or cure a fatty condition.

Second, a farmer's cows, pigs, and chickens would grow thin, if fed only with fat foods. Every farmer knows that he needs foods which will ferment like malt in a brewery - sour mushy brans or swill - to fatten animals.

Third, Eskimos live on fat foods the year around, eating almost nothing but fat - mostly blubber, which is the fattest of fat foods - yet, they are not stout.

They take little exercise; in fact, during the long Arctic winters - 10 months of each year - there is practically NO exercise. Yet, they do not become fat.
They eat no foods which ferment and produce the frothy brewery like ferment, such as is produced in the human body by fermentation in the stomach and small intestine.

Fermentation is the one important cause of fatness.
Purification is the one and permanent remedy for stoutness or fatness.
It allows one to eat what one needs and what one wants.

Abnormal fatness and excessive stoutness are usually water bloat. So-called fatness is water lodged in between the cells of the body. It is left there by the blood in an attempt to counteract the poison of acids due to filthy fermenting acids.

Ten thousand clean ripe strawberries fresh from the garden are pure strawberries, because they contain those substances which are native to themselves.
But if you soak those strawberries in vinegar, alcohol, and kitchen slops, and leave them in such a mixture for a month, not one of the, will be pure.

Ten billion bodily cells, living in their natural alkaline solutions, are pure. But if you let them soak for months or years in sour acids - fermenting fluid wastes of the body, not one of those ten billion cells will be healthy.

A body is pure, when it contains only that which is normal unto itself.

The pure chemistry of every cell of the human body is predominately alkaline.

Alkalies and acids are the chemical opposites of each other.

Soda is alkaline. Vinegar is an acid. They neutralize each other. Put a little soda in a glass; pour in a little vinegar. The mixture is neither alkali nor acid.

Alkalies destroy acids and acids destroy alkalies. This is one of the evidences of God's wisdom so that both vegetable life and animal life will be preserved. If alkalies become too strong, acids neutralize them; if acids become too strong, alkaline fluids neutralize the acids - except when man's ignorance upsets the balance.

God made creation thus - to perfect the circle of the Great Truth of Life.

Some vegetable cells thrive in acid solutions, even in rotting solution.

But cells of the human body are healthy only when living in alkaline solutions.

Cell tissues of man are healthy only when predominately alkaline.

A vegetable may thrive on rotting acid slops, but when man tries to live like a vegetable, the acids tend to eat up his tissue, or rot or bloat it.

Acidosis is the term used to designate the condition which exists when fluids of the body tend to become acidulent. Such a condition always leads to poisoning.

Such poisoning is called Toxemia. Self-poisoning is called auto-intoxication.

All diseases - both germ diseases and non-germ diseases, as well as feebleness, nervousness, old age, death - are due in part to an over-amount of impure acids.

Over acidity, due to fermentation and a rotting condition in the body, produces perfect 'soil' for all infectious disease germs. Unless some over-acidity has provided food and soil for germs, NO germ disease can exist in the body.

"There is invariably a state of Acidosis as a foundation upon which infections are grafted - - unless they (patients) get rid of acidosis, Toxemia is sure to follow, and that Toxemia will soon get rid of them.(1)

Waste materials which solidify in the body form only one form of impurity.

Impurities in liquid form can circulate about the body as deadly poisons.

————

(1) George K. Bell, M.D., New York, Polyclinic Hospital.

Life depends on the body remaining in a normally alkaline condition.

All tissues of the body - cells and liquids - organs, blood, secretions, are normal only when slightly alkaline. Alkalinity keeps the body healthy and youthful.

On the other hand, surplus acids are the enemies of the human tissues and cells; in fact, any kind of acid tends to eat up animal tissues.

When I state that acids eat up animal tissues, I mean just that.

Even the mild acid of lemon juice or sour milk eats skin cells to such a degree, that - when used - it eats off enough skin to let out the pigment of freckles.

Carbolic acid is stronger. It will eat great holes into human flesh.

Every acid - mild or strong - tends to eat up cells of the human body, and every over-amount of acid interferes with the natural physiological processes of the body.

Over-acidity is impurity. Acidosis results in poisoning; poisoning in death.

Pure blood is strongly alkaline. If the blood loses even a little of its alkalinity, it becomes impure - loaded with poisonous acids. The injection of even a very little acid into the blood, will greatly lower the vitality of an animal.

If such injections are repeated daily for a number of days, the result is death.

Yet, if alkaline salts are injected into the blood to counteract the acid, the animal comes back to health and vitality, even though it was very near to death.

Acids eat up the human tissues; they eat up the muscle cells; they eat up the nerve cells; they eat up bone structure. X-ray photographs of the bones of a person who has suffered from rheumatism due to acidity, shows clearly that acids actually eat into the ends of bones at the joints. Such a bone-eaten condition exists wherever chronic rheumatism due to acidity - or any other trouble due to acidosis - has become localized in hand, foot, knee, elbow, shoulder, hip, thigh or back.

Nature always tries to save an individual from poisoning himself to death.

When poisonous acids saturate any part of the body - liver, kidneys, or other glands, nerve paths, muscles, or bone ends at joints - nature does one of three things, or all three, to save the person from immediate death.

When acids begin to saturate cell tissues, nature - to save the individual from death - (a) turns the acids into crystals, hardening them so that they can no longer soak into surrounding cells and poison them to death; or (b) nature tries to use up the acids by growing ulcers and tumors; or (c) nature dilutes the acids with so much water that they are not strong enough to actually kill the body at once.

Let us learn how nature uses each of these methods.

First, when nature solidifies the acids, it turns them into little long, hard, white,needle-like, glass-like crystals. If in the muscle then - with every movement at a joint - the crystals cut the tissue like little ripping needles.
If such a localization of needle-like crystals - almost as hard as glass - becomes chronic, excess sodium and urea may combine and produce arthritis, or else lay the basis for it. It is hardening and stiffening of the joints of which the exact cause is little known, except that without acidosis, then neuritis appears.
If in secreting organs, the crystals are rounded, and called 'stones'.

Second, when acids collect in great quantities in certain parts of the body, nature produces tumors, ulcers, cancers, et cetera. Tumors use up the waste acids. Nature knows it is wiser to produce a tumor in one place, than to kill the entire body.

Third, when nature finds that the entire body is being saturated almost unto death with the poisonous acids due to fermentation and fil- thy conditions within the body, nature drains all the water possible from other organs, and then pours this extra water into the blood so that the blood can let it soak in between the cells of the body,diluting and weakening the acids which would otherwise eat the cells alive.

It is this water-bloat which produces most of the fatness of today.
Nature prefers to bloat the body, rather than let it be poisoned to death.

Bloating is usually called stoutness. The fat of most fat people of today is nothing but water bloat - extra water used to dilute poisons kept within the body.

Even though you may not use enough sense to get rid of such acids, your bodily intelligence causes glands and muscular tissues to drain themselves and pour more water into the blood, so that your blood can leave more water in between cells to dilute the poisonous acids. Thus your body becomes bloated and fat.

Of every ten thousand fat people, there is not more than one case of real fat.

A fat person should sing praises unto the Lord thus: "Even though I am too dirty and lazy to keep clean inside, and even though my body is like a filthy frothing fermenting beer vat, yet, I praise the Lord that the cells of my body are intelligent enough to bloat up my body with water to dilute its poisons, and save me from death."

Since all cells are fed by the blood, anything which tends to lessen the amount of acid in the blood helps to save the life of the cells of the body.

And, any acid substance which weakens the blood's alkalinity, renders it impure and unfit to furnish those salts on which the life of the cells depends.

Carbonic acid gas is a waste of the body and very poisonous to the body.

When blood is normally alkaline, it carries 20% of its own volume in carbonic acid gas from the cells, to the lungs, so that breathing gets rid of that poison.

But when the alkalinity of the blood is reduced even slightly, it is able to carry only 3% of its volume in carbonic acid gas, and the remaining 17% must remain in the tissues of the body, poisoning them to the point of death.

Dr. Walters studied the weakened alkalinity of the blood of rabbits due to mild use of acid of lemon juice. When so weakened that it could carry only 3% of carbonic acid gas, the rabbits were so near death that they were (a) unable to move, (b) could scarcely breathe, and (c) were almost unable to keep up heart action.

But when Dr. Walters injected alkaline salt into their blood, the blood was able to carry the normal amount of carbonic acid gas away from the tissues, and the rabbits were restored to life, activity and permanent health.

Besides feeding cells and carrying away wastes, the blood kills disease germs.

Disease germs can exist as a danger to the body only when the blood's alkalinity is weakened by acid impurities.

NO disease germ can continue to exist in the blood, when it is normally alkaline.

Dr. Von Foder cured rabbits which were known to be infected - some with cholera germs, some with typhoid germs, some with tuberculosis germs.

He increased the alkalinity of the blood by daily use of sodium carbonate; and the diseases did not develop, although virulent germs were previously present.

Other rabbits were ill with the same diseases. Their blood was not kept normally alkaline. In them, diseases developed rapidly, and were fatal in nearly every case.

But when animals were even near to death, disease germs were killed, and the animals recovered, when the blood was made alkaline.

Poisonous saturation can produce extreme thinness or filthy bloated fatness.

If you, with power of life and death, were absolute emperor over millions of people working loyally for you, would you day by day slyly poison them until they became so thin, that they shriveled up with skin stretched splittingly over their bones?

Or, if you were god of this world, would you flood your entire earth and submerge a billion individuals in diluted watery poisons, actually drowning a thousand million individuals, until their bodies swelled and bloated beyond recognition?

If you would and do, it's no wonder you become fat.

I care not if you are shocked. I know your soul does not want to permit such a condition. The soul is pure; but I am writing to help you to purify your body.

Oh, purify your body. Free it of those deadly acids which produce kidney troubles, liver troubles, heart trouble, brain fag, make infectious germs diseases possible, and when crystallized, produce rheumatism; and when diluted, produce fat.

When you purify your body, its cells will not be half-drowned in poisonous wastes, and you will be vibrant with health and buoyant with youthfulness.

Then you will not have to sleep eight hours a day.
And you cannot be exceedingly thin, and you cannot be fat or stout.

The next Lesson takes up sources of acids, and means of remedying acidosis - for it is necessary for us to know (a) the sources of these acids and poisons, (b) how to prevent the body from producing them, (c) how to dissolve those which have crystallized; and (d) how to purify the body by washing such poisons out of it.

LESSON VII - IF WE WASH OUT THE FERMENT, MAY WE NOT LIVE FOREVER?

Man, so complexly made, is still the most divine unity in all creation.

No process works by itself alone, - as fatigue poisons accumulate, more cells break down and produce disintegrative wastes, as well as acids and fatigue poisons.

Then also as acid wastes increase, cells tire and wear out more quickly so that more fatigue and disintegrative wastes are added to the acid poisons.

The entire body acts as a unit; that is why I give major attention first to the substances which make the body impure, and now give major attention to the four great means of purification. Since each means frees the body of several different wastes, you can now aid each means in its work of purification.

So now study (a) the source of acid poisons in the body - whatever form, whether in crystal or fluid form; (b) how to stop production of abnormal acids in the body; (c) how to dissolve the crystals, and (d) how to free the body of acid saturating the body.

The abnormal acids in the body come from three general sources:
First, some acids are taken into the body as foods and drink.
Second, others result from physiological functioning and death of cells;
Third, still other acids are manufactured in the body by fermentation.

First: Acids are taken into the body by every food which tastes 'sour'.
Sweet apples, plums, apricots, and even pears contain about one three-hundredth part of acid. Most berries contain approximately one per centum of pure acid. Lemons, limes, and grapefruit contain from seven to fifteen per centum of acid.
Also acids are taken into the body by rhubarb and tomatoes, and by various food combinations - such as salads, sauerkraut, cold slaw, in fact, by all sour foods.

Second: Acids are produced in the body by its physiological activities. But such acids are taken care of normally if the blood is kept in an alkaline condition, if skin and lungs are kept active, and kidneys and intestines work properly.

Even wearing down of cell structure in the ordinary work tends to produce acids.

Such acids tend to accumulate at the center of the cell.

Unless neutralized by alkaline salts fed to the cell by alkaline blood, the acid in the course of time, eats up the center or brain of the cell.

The continued life of every bodily cell depends on securing enough alkaline salts to neutralize the acid which tends to accumulate at its center. Blood must supply each cell - no matter where located - with the kinds of salts which that cell needs to neutralize the particular acids accumulating at its cell center.

Alkaline salts are the only substances which can be assimilated by a cell to neutralize the acid at its center, and prevent the acid from eating it alive.

Third, digestive fermentation is the great source of poisonous acids manufactured in the body. Such acids murderously eat up the cells.

Fermentation is souring. In the body, it is usually due to mixing sugars and starches, or starches and acids, at the same meal.

Acids manufactured within the body - especially in stomach and small intestine - are much more powerful than the acids taken into the body as foods.

Moreover, the production of such acids may continue every hour of the day, day after day for years. It is a continuous process - like the production of acids and filthy scum in breweries which run night and day, year after year.

If you have ever tried making home brew, or even old fashioned root beer, you know how starches and sugars ferment. With water, billions of germs develop in mixtures of acids and starches, or of sugars and starches, and stinking scum rises to the surface. In breweries, this is skimmed off hour by hour, but in the stomach, such skimming cannot be done. The sour acids, bubbles, gases, and filthy froth are due to the alcohol and carbonic acid gas produced by fermentation.

Fermentation is the greatest source of the poisonous acids of the body.

And whenever acid foods are eaten with starch foods, starches begin to ferment, producing acids, alcohol, swill, and gas.

Acid fruits stop digestion in the stomach before the alkaline salts of such fruits are freed. No matter how beneficial the alkaline salts are, after they reach the blood, it is indigestion of starches caused by the acids of fruits and vegetables eaten with starch foods, which leads to fermentation.

Yet, even though acid fruits hinder or stop digestion of starch foods, acid fruits should be eaten, because their alkaline salts are very beneficial.

There is unquestionable scientific proof of the fact that even a mild acid eaten with starch foods, actually delays digestion and starts fermentation.

Combine starch solution with 1% of saliva, and the starch is changed into maltose in four minutes. This is the first step in normal starch digestion.

But if you add only 1/20,000 part of oxalic acid (the acid in tomatoes) the process of changing the starch into maltose will be delayed 19 minutes, or nearly five times as long as the normal four minute period.

Or if you add 1% of lemon juice, the digestion of the starch food will be stopped for 42 minutes.

Or if you add 1/50th part of mediumly sweet apple juice, digestion of starches will be delayed for 45 minutes.

Yet, acid fruits are of great value.

This sounds like a conundrum but things are not what they seem: (a) starch foods, which taste neither sweet nor sour, manufacture deadly acid and sour poisons; (b) acid fruits provide alkaline salts for the blood; (c) sugar which does not taste sour produces both alcohol and sour acids; and (d) every swallow of sweet milk taken by an adult sours within two minutes after it reaches the stomach.

Yet, even though acid fruits hinder starch digestion, nevertheless I do advise you to eat such acid fruit and vegetables. Later I explain when they should be eaten to obtain the benefits, and yet prevent accumulation of those impure acids within the body which poison nerve centers and eat up cell structure.

To stop the manufacture of deadly acids produced by fermentation:
First, neutralize the ferment which exists in stomach and intestine.
When there is an acid ferment which has been left in the stomach day after day, use just what God intended you to use as a food to counteract the ferment.
God put alkaline substances in the body - in the blood and in every secretion of every gland - to neutralize acids. God created alkaline foods to neutralize acids.

Hence, when needed, use the best substances God created to neutralize acids.
If you have been so stupid as to create a chronic sour fermenting stomach and indigestion has set in - much like the ferment of hops and malt in a brewery - then use a little baking soda morning and night, or even before and after every meal. Soda is a real food; not a medicine. It is an alkaline food. Use a little baking soda in water to stop the fermenting and putrifying in the stomach and intestine.

Use about as much soda as you can pile up on a ten cent piece; dissolve it in a half glass of water; and drink it a half hour before eating; and a like amount after each meal.

Second, cleanse the stomach and small intestine.
Acid fruits are the very best food cleansers we have.
There is no food or medicine which equals acid fruits as cleansers.
But since they are cleansers, they should be used as a cleanser.

To illustrate: To cook an Irish Stew, you put a kettle on the stove. You find the kettle dirty, because it has not been used for some time. You wish to clean it. So you use clean hot water and 99½% pure soap. These are the best cleaners for cleaning the inside of the kettle.

Certainly you do not clean the kettle and cook the stew at the same time. You do not mix water and soap with vegetables and meats for the stew.

Instead, you use water and soap first as cleaners to perform their function after their kind. Then you cook the foods to make the stew after their kind.

So use as much sense in cleaning and feeding the body as you use in cleaning a kettle and cooking an Irish stew.
Make a complete meal of acid fruits or acid fruit juices, with nothing else.
Use them as cleansers, but do not mix your cleansing acid fruits with starch foods, any more than you would mix soap and water with the ingredients of your stew.

Certainly do use acid fruits - oranges, grapefruit, et cetera, and the acid vegetables, rhubarb and tomatoes. Use them (a) because they contain alkaline salts which when taken into the blood, counteract the acids which have been lodged in the joints, or which tend to saturate the blood or soak into the cell tissues of the body; use them (b) because they are rich in vitamins; and use them (c) because they are ideal cleansers when used alone as cleansers.

Third, stop providing foods for fermentation - or rather stop combining foods so that they will start and continue fermentation.
Every acid food, if eaten with any starch food of any kind, hinders or stops the digestion of the starch foods, and starts fermentation.
Fermentation always produces gas and sour acids, alcohol and frothy swill.
Even the acid of a sweet apple, delays starch digestion for half an hour.
So acid fruits and sour foods should not be combined with starch foods. Combined means cooked together, or eaten at the same meal.
Foods are combined in the stomach if eaten within an hour or two of each other.
Of course, no individual wants to eat acid foods with starch foods unless his body is already so poisoned with wastes that nature demands something to stop digestion so that his blood will not be overloaded with more food.

To dissolve acid crystals which are lodged in the body:

First, use juices of acid fruits, preferably orange juice, either late at night or early in the morning, or both night and morning.

The juice of one orange in a half glass of distilled water is enough.

If taken in the morning, take it at least one hour before breakfast.

Second, use distilled water as drinking water. It is the most powerful solvent which can be taken into the body without harm to the tissues of the body. It is of greater value than any other substance in reducing over-fatness and dissolving acid crystals in any part of the body.

Third, when acids have crystallized at joints, or in muscles, don't rub the part - for rubbing presses the crystals deeper into the flesh and cuts it.

Fourth, wash the skin of the affected part with an Epsom Salts bath - a tablespoonful of salts to a pint of hot water, and gently dry the skin with your hand.

Fifth, anoint the skin over the joint or affected part with vaseline. Great claims are made for many oils, but none are so valuable as vaseline.

Sixth, when acids have been turned into acid crystals and lodged in certain parts of the body, pat the part to keep the blood in circulation, after having washed the skin over the affected part, and oiled it. Don't rub, but - with the palms of your hands pat - pat, pat - the part affected, patting it gently and rhythmically.

Thus you will help to free the acid crystals, stimulate the circulation, and press out the waste acids soaked in around and between the cells.

To neutralize and absorb the acid fluids which saturate any part of the body, producing fat, or rather bloat:

First, bathe the part twice daily with Epsom Salts bath -½3 tablespoonfuls of salts to a quart of hot water. Dry the skin with your hands, not with a towel.

Second, if the part is especially fat and saggy, double the amount of salts and water, and - wringing out a small towel in it - apply the hot towel for half a minute at a time to the part. Repeat eight or ten times each morning and night.

Third, to neutralize the acids which cause water bloat (or fat) use iodized salt in your distilled drinking water. You can buy Iodized salt at a good grocery. Use just a bit to flavor the water to suit taste.

Purify your body of crystals and frothy swill, and be born again - as energetic, youthful, and slender and trim, as you were at 20.

BODY PURIFICATION

By

Brown Landone

LESSON VIII - "BE THOU CLEAN!"

Keep the great vision: Physiologists - even materialists - frankly admit that if we did not foolishly allow impurities to accumulate in the body, and if we did not stupidly manufacture other impurities in the body, we should live forever.

Continued youthfulness is merely continued purity of the body.

With our prejudices of social conventions, some subjects seem disagreeable for discussion. Such prejudices are peculiar and local. In England, one may freely talk of ones bowels, but one must never utter the word 'stomach'. Americans hesitate to use the word bowels. Be pure of mind. Regard elimination of impurities from kidneys and intestines as you regard breathing which eliminates wastes from the lungs.

Great scientists declare that if we kept the large intestine sweet and clean, there could be no hardening of the arteries. It is poison absorbed from the intestine which causes blood to leave mineral salts and other wastes in the artery walls, which results in high blood pressure, and makes old age and early death certain.

Of course, a great mass of undigested food goes into the large intestine - for "part of the food is never absorbed into the body, it is indigestible - - - instances of this are vegetable fibers, partially or poorly utilized proteins, such as those found in lentils, and seeds of plants." (1)

Such a mass of undigested food is necessary in both small and large intestine. They are about 26 feet long, and the large intestine is two inches in diameter. Food must furnish bulk on which the muscle fibers of the large intestine can act.

I could carry enough chemically condensed food tablets in my vest pocket to last for several weeks. But if I used such food for six months, I would become insane or die, for if the intestine had nothing within it to cause its muscles to act, its blood would over flood the brain, and I would become insane or die of apoplexy.

So for bulk, it is wise to eat quantities of food which will not digest, and which will not ferment or putrify, or paste up the walls of the large intestine.

Intestinal ills of today are due to rapid dietetic changes. The starchy potato, native to Peru, was not generally used by the white man until 200 years ago. Our corn was not an internationally known food until after our war of 1812. Not a single bushel of refined flour or wheat, or barley, or rye, was ever made before 1870.

_____

(1) "Physiology" p 216, by V. H. Mottram.

And sugar consumption has increased more than 1000% in the last 100 years. We have changed from meat and green leaf foods to a sugar and starch diet.

It is eating of quantities of sugars and starches to provide bulk, instead of the old green leaf products which we once used, which poisons the intestine.

"The profession is only just beginning to realize the - - fouling of the food supply, and the poisoning and deterioration of the tissues by septic material absorbed from the intestine. These noxious substances getting into the circulation are carried away to every organ and tissue in the body, and produce disastrous results in proportion to the degree of the toxicity of the blood." (2)

Most ill conditions - from sick headaches to cancer - are initiated by ill conditions in the intestine.

"Abnormal conditions of the intestines are largely responsible for the common headache malady and for a generally lowered resistence, resulting in acids - and even more serious ailments." (3)

One great scientist (4) believes that intestinal poisoning is the cause of ulcers, of small intestine, and cancers of breasts, colon and stomach.
"In chronic intestinal stasis active patheogenic bacteria thrive in the bowels - - a very potent influence in favoring the occurrence of cancer." (5)
"All creatures automatically poison themselves - - not time, but these toxic products, produce these senile changes which we call old age." (6)

Every waste kept in the large intestine longer than it should be retained, (a) pastes up the walls of the large intestine and impacts it, or (b) continues fermentation started in the small intestine and impacts it, or (c) starts putrification (rotting) and develops billions of disease germs in the large intestine.
So long as these multiply there are foul odors and gases in the large intestine, and their poisons are absorbed into the blood.

Of germs in the large intestine, I quote only conservative scientists.

"In the intestine the number of bacteria increases progressively - - the large intestine swarming with them." (7)
"Every twenty minutes, each normal germ gives birth to another by dividing itself into two - - at this rate each microbe becomes the ancestor of more than seven million germs every twenty four hours." (8)
"Countless billions of poisonous germs - - invade the intestinal tract." (9)

(2) Sir Arbuthnot Lane, London, Surgeon to the Kind.
(3) "How to Live," p 68, by E. L. Fisk, M.D.
(4) Sir G. L. Cheatle, Fellow of Royal College of Surgeons, London.
(5) British Medical Journal, by A. T. Jordon, M.D.
(6 - 8) James Empringham, M.D.
(9) "The Human Body" p 61 by Logan Glendening, M.D.

"The stool is normally by bulk about 1/3 bacteria." (10)
(The stool means the amount of waste evacuated by large intestine.)
"Bacteria multiply so rapidly that about half the contents of the lower intestine are bacteria, excreted at the rate of about 130,000,000, 000,000 a day." (11)
"Need we wonder that the average human colon is at all times a cesspool of billions of toxic bacteria, continually polluting the blood stream with such poisons, as indol, phenol, skatol, and many others." (12)

The intestine becomes a filthy breeding cesspool, not so much because of the kinds of food we now eat, but because of the way we combine them.

We modern people eat more starches than any race has ever eaten in all history. Then also we are the great sugar eating race of all ages.
Sugar consumed per person in the U.S. is greater than anywhere else in the world; and the amount of starch we consume is greater per person than in rice eating in China.

Now note the relative work of digesting starch foods and sugar foods.

Starch, when properly digested is changed into sugar. It takes 20 hours to digest starches - that is, 20 hours of work, for nature to turn starches into sugars.

But sugars - all sweets - can be dissolved in the digestive tract and passed into the blood in 10 minutes. Some sugars show in the blood in 3 minutes.

Nature is not a fool, and will not do unnecessary work.
The large amount of sugars we eat today usually supplies all that the body needs of that kind of food.
So when starches and sugars are eaten at the same meal, the starch is seldom digested. When we over-eat large quantities of starch and sugar, the body with a few minutes work can obtain all that it needs of that kind of food from the sugar. So why should it do a hundred and twenty times more work, merely to change starch into sugar of which it already has a plentiful supply?

Nature is not a fool. Consequently, with large amounts of starches and sugars, nature uses the sugar, and leaves starches undigested.

Undigested starches either ferment, or form a gluey paste.
When starch is mixed with water in the large intestine, it forms a paste. When we eat so much sugar, the starch foods are not digested. Then the undigested starches pass on to the large intestine and form a paste - a paste, gluey enough to stick for 10 years, or even for a life time.

_____

(10) "The Human Body" by Logan Glendening, M.D.
(11) "Why We Behave Like Human Beings" by G. A. Dorsey
(12) James Empringham, M.D.

This produces what is called "Impaction" of the large intestine.

Post mortem examinations reveal immense amounts of thick hardened starch glue, pasted on the inside of the large intestine. A London surgeon has preserved a large intestine stretched to 20 inches in diameter, which contained nearly three gallons of waste starch paste, weighing 20 pounds. That helps to create bay-window abdomens.

Post mortems were made of the bodies of 100 men and women of New York slums. These people had lived active lives, and had not had 'rich' foods. Yet, each intestine was lined with paste from 1/4 to 1 inch thick. Similar conditions were found by an eminent European surgeon (13) who performed 2,000 post mortems.

The condition is general. Fluroscopy and the x-ray reveal that even people who seem to be in excellent health have impacted intestines.

Any one, whose abdomen sticks out more than it did when the person was fourteen years of age, has some impaction.

Regular intestinal movement once a day is no proof of no-impactment. There may be a pastey coating an inch thick, and yet the daily undigested matter will be evacuated, leaving the waste paste glued to the inner wall of the intestine.

This makes the ill results of such a condition evident. Some physicians state that disease could not exist, if the intestines were kept clean and pure.

In general, such ill results are of three kinds.
First, pressure on other organs, caused by the weight of such great masses of impacted material in the large intestine.
Second, poisoning of the blood due to absorption of toxins.
Third, breeding of bacteria and disease germs which are carried by the blood to all parts of the body.

The pressure: When an intestine contains two gallons or 16 pounds of this impacted waste, its weight exerts enough pull to cause misplacement or prevent normal functioning (a) of the bladder and urinary tract in both sexes, (b) of the womb in the woman, and (c) of the prostate gland in man. Moreover, such abnormal weight pressing on the sex nerve centers causes over-excitation or deadening - for we now know that the sacral ganglia, through branches of one and the same nerve, serves the rectum, the bladder and the sex organs.

Many chronic misplacements in women, and prostatic inflammation in men, have been remedied by removing intestinal impaction.

_____

(13) Nathan Mutch, M.D., Guy's Hospital, London.

THE POISONING: Impaction causes the semi-fluid waste poisons to be retained in the intestine. And as each ounce of blood in the body flows through the capillaries of the large intestine several times every 24 hours, chronic poisoning in the intestine keeps up a continuous poisoning of the blood.

THE BREEDING: of billions of poisonous germs: Decaying impacted waste in the intestine provides the best breeding ground for disease germs. Disease germs grow rapidly; they pass easily into the blood and are carried throughout the body - lodging wherever the body is least able to fight them.

Germ diseases cannot develop unless there is acidosis and intestinal poisoning. Even cancer is now associated with poisons absorbed from the large intestine.
"There are many diseases - - - which are no more than symptoms of chronic intestinal stasis - - - percolations from the (intestinal) cesspool - - - the whole body becomes inhabited - - by disease." (14)

HOLD TO THE GREAT VISION: The soul is perfect with unlimited energy. Only impurities in the body prevent its continued youthfulness.

If you weigh 150 pounds, would you do your work easily and with joy if you had to pull around ten times your weight in lead - 1500 pounds?

Your stomach weighs one pound. How can it supply your body with well digested food to give you energy, if pulled down by intestinal impaction of ten pounds?

Is it any wonder you lack energy?

When you free yourself of such a condition, you free yourself not only of poisons, but of pounds of weight which actually pulls organs out of place and prevents them from doing their work to give you the energy and joy you want in life.

Scientists have positively asserted that if we did not allow impurities to accumulate in the body, our bodies should live forever.

Hold to the vision, and fulfill it. Dissolve and wash out the mineral walls built up between the cells in your body; dissolve the sharp acid crystals and wash them out of your body; breathe out waste fatigue poisons so that you can enjoy life twenty hours a day; and purify the intestine which you have allowed to become a filthy cesspool, so that it shall be free of foul odors and putrifying wastes.

In next Lesson, I give you methods of purifying it and keeping it pure.

------

(14) Leonard Williams, M.D., French Hospital, London.

By
Brown Landone

LESSON IX - TEACH THE INTESTINE TO "THINK" IN ACTION

In many ancient religions, the number seven was the sacred symbol of purity; spiritual leaders called the people to the Temple for purification every seventh day; and - most surprising - the means used symbolized the purification of the body.

These are seven means of intestinal purification. Three to be used to purify the intestinal tract of wastes already existing in it, and four to re-awaken activity of the intestinal walls so that they will continue the purifying process.

I give the first three in this Lesson; the other four in the next Lesson.

FIRST, STOP SUPPLYING the large intestine with an over load of foods which ferment and putrify. Stop eating too much starch; stop eating too much sugar; stop eating too much sugar and starch at the same meal or within two or three hours of each other. Instead, eat quantities of green leaf products.

SECOND, stop the multiplication of germs which cause deadly putrification.

There are two kinds of germs in the large intestine. One is vegetative; the other is an animal form. The animal germ is poisonous. The vegetable germ is beneficial - it helps to kill off the animal germs. That is the reason Metchnikoff received the idea of attaining eternal youth by drinking sour milk - for sour milk contains the vegetable germs which destroy the putrifying germs.

But now we know that very few of the beneficial germs taken in sour milk - the vegetable germs which destroy the putrifying germs - ever reach the intestine alive. They are themselves digested before they reach it.

Yet, there is a very simple means - a food substance which will, if taken a glassful at night, or a glassful in the morning, cleanse and purify the intestine - change it from a dangerous cesspool of putrifying germs, to a clean sweet-odored colon.

Oh, don't turn up your nose at sauer kraut juice.

Great good often comes from lowly and despised things. Christ was born in a mule's feed box; and even wise men said, "Can any good come out of Nazareth?"

Since sauer kraut juice will help to kill the putrifying germs, use it. If you do not happen to like the taste of the juice - what of it? Salt and pepper it; use a drop or two of Worcester Sauce if you wish. Add whatever will make it tasty to you.

Third, clean out any old waste impacted or pasted in the intestines.

But don't follow any such advice as that of taking a colon flushing for six or eight nights in succession. Any such advice is due to well-intentioned ignorance.

Many physicians object to intestinal flushing or washing, because it has been so misused. It is right to object to its mis-use; but it is silly to object to it on the ground that it is 'abnormal' and 'unnatural'.

Never be afraid of the words abnormal and unnatural; I have never known a medical physician that is positive he knew what he meant when he used them.

When anyone insists that I can reach the highest attainment only by using that which is 'natural' I marvel at his stupidity.

I do not wish to go back to nature. I wish to go on to God. If we should try to go back to nature, we would have to give up all automobiles, railways, steamships, telephones, and electric lights; towels, and soaps; all newspapers and books; all knives and forks; all radios and violins; all colleges, churches, and art galleries.

Nothing but stupidity leads anyone to want to go back to nature.

So, when a physician or health specialist advises against the use of a colon flushing because it is not natural or normal, I know that he does so because he has known the evils of its misuse, but has NO reason for objecting to its real use.

But, anyway, even colon flushings are natural. Many animals when ill go to a pool or river, and by suction draw water up into the rectum and then expel it. It is an exceptional means, used to relieve an abnormal condition.

When abnormal conditions exist, exceptional means should be used.

Certainly, I do not keep the back of my neck always covered with camphor ice. But, after two or three days' bathing and sunburn in early summer, the skin on my neck is abnormally blistered and raw. To relieve such an abnormal condition, I use an exceptional means - even plastering the skin with camphor ice.

So also, whenever an abnormally impacted condition exists in the intestine, it is divinely right to use an exceptional means to loosen and remove such impaction.

Intestinal flushing is by far the best means of accomplishing this.

The intestinal bath should NOT be continuously used; it should be used only as an exceptional means to remedy an abnormal condition. Mis-use or over-use of the intestinal bath will lessen the activity of the muscles of the large intestine. So I do not advise continued use; not even frequent use.

However, after years of observation of its value to others, and collection of much evidence, I know that even colon flushing is the best method of quickly relieving an impacted condition of the large intestine - easily and thoroughly - if used as I advise its use; and I know that the method I suggest differs from all other methods of which I have known. It actually develops the activity of the muscle walls of the intestine, instead of lessening their impulse to action.

This method I originated about thirty years ago and published a little booklet about it. It has been used in hundreds of cases, and in each case it has helped to develop and stimulate the muscle fibers, of the intestine, instead of deadening their activity. That is why I urge you to follow the directions which follow.

AS TO THE FLUSHING BAG: There are many different kinds of colon flushing bags. The ordinary cheap fountain syringe bag is satisfactory. It is better than the more costly bags. It should be used without a 15 to 20 inch colon tube. Except when inserted by a physician or a nurse, the colon tube is likely to be more harmful than beneficial, if you attempt to insert such a tube yourself, it seldom passes the S-like bend of your intestine. Being of elastic material, it bends back, redoubles on itself, so that the tube coils up in the lower portion of your intestine. It is only when the pressure of the soil or the water becomes great enough to distend the S-like bend, that the tube will pass up into the ascending colon. This stretches and distends the muscle walls of the intestine without stimulating them to action. So do not try to use the colon tube unless you are helped by a nurse or physician.

I now answer several questions usually asked: and then give you the method of using the intestinal bath, which re-awakens intestinal muscles to activity.

(a) the purpose of colon flushing is to loosen and remove impaction of the intestines which has existed for a considerable time.

(b) The amount of water should never be more than can be taken with ease. Use only enough to cause a desire of the muscle walls of the intestine to expel it. Then you work with the intelligence of the muscle walls of the intestine, instead of stretching them contrary to their impulse to act.

Do not attempt to use any designated amount of water; do not try to retain the water for a specified time; and as soon as the muscles of the intestine 'feel' as though they should like to expel the water, let them do so. It is more important to let them respond to their impulse to activity, than to reatin the water.

(c) The TEMPERATURE of the water used should be warmer than the blood, because it will then more readily dissolve the starchy paste. Some German physicians advise very cold water; others advise very hot water. Use water just warm enough to feel agreeable to your hand.

(d) DIFFERENT SUBSTANCES may be used in the water, each to meet a particular need, and to accomplish a result after its own kind.

If there is a stringy cream colored mucus in the fecal matter, a very weak soapy water may be used. A few drops of Synol Liquid soap to a quart of water is sufficient.

If there is considerable gas in the intestine, use about one-half teaspoonful of Zonite to each quart of clear water.

If you feel especially tired when taking the intestinal bath, a half teaspoonful of iodized table salt can be added to each quart of clear water.

If the fecal matter of the preceding two or three days has been very hard, a quarter teaspoonful of Epsom Salts can be added to each quart of water, providing the salts are thoroughly dissolved before the water is used for flushing the colon.

Now we come to the two new factors of greatest importance - the two factors which change the effect of the intestinal bath from weakening the intestinal muscles, to stimulating and strengthening them in accord with their impulse to act.

The first of these two factors, I call 'positional relaxation'.
The second of the two factors, I call 'related breathing'.

The position of the body in taking the intestinal bath is very important.

Many different positions have been recommended; (a) to lie flat on the back with the knees flexed; (b) to take the knee and shoulder position; (c) to sit on a specially designed bag which costs several dollars, so that the weight of your body on the bag forces water up into the intestine. Use none of these.

FUNCTIONAL RELAXATION: Lie on your bed on your back, with feet spread some distance apart and slightly raised - resting on footboard of the bed for instance.

This relaxes all the muscles of the abdomen and allows the water to flow slightly downward, instead of being forced uphill as in the sitting position.

Or, if very tense and nervous, lie in a bathtub of hot water while taking the intestinal bath; let the warm water thoroughly relax the abdominal muscles before you begin to take the colon flushing.

RELATED BREATHING: This is the most important factor.
(a) Hold the tube of the colon flushing bag between your thumb and finger.
(b) Press it between thumb and finger so that NO water can flow into the intestine except when you release the pressure.
(c) Breathe slowly and easily with the upper part of the chest for a moment or two before you allow any water to flow into the intestine.

(d) Then, when breathing becomes rhythmic, release pressure of thumb and finger, and let the water flow into the intestine, while you exhale your breath.

(e) Next pinch with thumb and finger and stop flow of water while you inhale.

Continue thus, slowly and easily - keeping your attention on your breathing and on the alternating pressure and relaxation of your thumb and finger.

Every time you let air out of your lungs, press your thumb and finger together, so that no water flows into your intestine while breathing air into your lungs.

Do you not see the marvel of this? It is so simple. There is no pain and no griping because there is no forced stretching of the intestinal walls.

With this method I give you, when you breathe out, you tend to create emptiness in the abdomen. The diaphram wall between lungs and abdomen moves upward.

That gives a chance for the water to flow into the abdomen easily. There is cooperation - the lungs pull up and the water flows up at the same time.

But when you breathe in, you stop letting water flow into the intestine. For when you inhale air, the bottom of the lungs is pushed downward; and if you should try to let water flow into the intestine at such a time, its upward movement would fight against the downward action of the incoming breath.

So, let water flow into the intestine with each outgoing breath. And stop the inflow of water with each incoming breath.

This naturally functions the intestine by establishing a rhythm of action. The rhythmic flow and non-flow of water into the intestine brings the muscles of the intestinal walls into normal action and tends to increase their activity; and water can flow into the intestine, without any stress or strain.

Moreover, related breathing prevents resistance of the intestinal walls. Taking the intestinal bath in any other way, lessens their activity, by stretching them contrary to their normal impulse to act, and sets up resistance due to the stupidity of the usual attempt to force water into the intestine contrary to the action of the intestinal muscles.

More important even than loosening the impaction at first, is the re-awakening of the intelligence of the muscle cells of the intestinal walls, to respond to their impulse to expel the water when they feel like doing so.

By
Brown Landone

LESSON X - "LET" MIND INTELLIGENCE WORK IN THE INTESTINE

Constipation is habitual inactivity of the large intestine.

Usual remedies are drugs, or foods which act as laxatives and cathartics. Such remedies - whether drugs or foods - cause action but never cure constipation: (a) because laxatives and cathartics act on the small intestine, (b) because constipation is inactivity of the large intestine; (c) because a laxative or cathartic does not cause the intestine to act - it merely produces a flood of water to lessen the harm of the laxative or cathartic.

Of laxatives and cathartics - both drugs and foods - there is much to learn.

Some substances which we call foods are drugs; and many a substance which we call drugs are foods. Many things sold in drug stores are not drugs, but real foods. Some things bought in grocery stores are actually drugs.

Of large and small intestine, there is also something to learn.

The large intestine is short and big, with heavy muscle fibers in its walls to squeeze upon substances within it, force them along, and push them out of the body.

The small intestine is smaller and four times as long as the large intestine.

With infinite wisdom God made this inner lining of the small intestine of a very thin layer of cells, so that the blood on the outer side of these thin walls, can easily suck into itself, the digested food substances.

This thin lining is only about one-tenth as thick as the thinnest tissue paper. If it is eaten through by acids or scratched and cut, blood flows into the intestine, and you may then easily bleed to death from internal hemorrhages.

Hence, the small intestines take very intelligent care of its inner lining.

Every laxative or cathartic - whether a food or a drug - is an irritant to the delicate tissue cells of the inner lining of the small intestine.

Every time a laxative or cathartic comes in contact with it, the cells of the delicate lining cry out that they must not be eaten up, or the body will bleed to death. They cry to the blood for help and the blood sacrifices itself by letting its water be sucked through the thin walls into the small intestine, to weaken and dilute the laxative or cathartic and wash the irritant down into the large intestine, where it produces either a watery movement, or softens the waste to be evacuated.

Normally little cells of the lining of the small intestine, suck digested foods from the intestine into the blood, supplying the blood to feed the body.

But all laxatives and cathartics reverse this process.

They cause the cells to suck water from the blood into the small intestine to dilute and weaken the irritants of laxatives or cathartics.
This floods the intestine with water, but tends to dry the blood.
When water is taken from the blood, it tends to become feverish. Then when the watery-wash reaches the large intestine, the blood demands that some of its water be returned to it. So, some of the water is re-absorbed from the large intestine into the blood, and carries poisons with it.

Although laxatives and cathartics do not cure constipation, yet sometimes it is wise to use them to wash out wastes more harmful than the cathartics themselves. For such a purpose, is there any choice? Are some less harmful than others?

Physicians prescribe Epsom Slats, rhubarb, citrates, castor oil, etc.
Nature curists argue about the evils of such salts, powders and oils; and loudly praise the 'natural' effects of brans, prunes, and fruit juices.
But what is the difference in the action of these substances? Why do nature curists insist that the physician's oils and salts are of the devil, while his brans and citrus fruit juices are of God?
How does each work? Why does any substance irritate the small intestine?

First, all acids tend to eat up animal tissues. Whenever an acid comes in contact with an animal cell, it tries to eat up that cell. And naturally, whenever an acid comes in contact with such a cell, the cell tries to protect its own life.

Whenever you take any unusual amount of citrus fruit or any acid fruit juice, the acid tends to eat into the thin tissue walls of the small intestine. Then the cells of the intestinal walls, call on the blood to help them, and the blood lets the cells suck its water into the small intestine to dilute the acids, so that the acids shall not eat through the lining of the intestine and cause you to bleed to death.

And how do medical cathartics work, - castor oil for instance?
Castor oil is a fat. In the process of digestion in the small intestine, every fat is separated into glycerin and fatty acids. In being digested, castor oil frees acid. Its acid tends to eat animal tissue, just as the acid of citrus fruits.

Consequently, when castor oil frees its acid in the small intestine, the cells of its inner lining cry out to the blood, asking for some of its water to dilute the acid. The blood responds, and helps to wash out the acids.

Real knowledge reveals that, in causing watery intestinal movements, the action of quantities of acid juices of fruit and the action of castor oil is the same.

Why argue about the evils of castor oil, and about the benefits of prunes and lemon juice and rhubarb sauce? One is no more natural than the other.

Never decide on the use of anything because it is called 'natural.'

Sweat pressed out of sweat glands is natural sweat; olive oil pressed out of olives is natural olive oil; castor oil pressed out of castor beans is natural castor oil; urine pressed out by the kidneys is natural urine.

Anyone urging this or that, because it is natural, is stupidly ignorant.

Faddists are reviving herb teas, as means of curing constipation.

Herb teas are made from stems and leaves, containing acid, sulphur, iron, et cetera. They are dark because of the green-black coloring matter of the leaves.

One woman I know, sets aside three days each month for use of an herb tea to clean herself out, and cure constipation - that is, for 3 days each month.

"It is wonderful," she says, "for two or three days after I take it, the most foul smelling material passes from my intestine. Why, it is actually green and black, which proves that it is just what I need to clean out my intestine."

Of course, the fecal matter which she evacuates is green and black because it is colored with the coloring matter of stem or of the leaves of the herb tea. And the fecal matter smells foul because of the acid, iron and sulphur.

Herb teas do possess valuable salts and vitamins; but they are not cures for constipation. They act just as castor oil and fruit juices act.

Yet, constipation can be easily cured - by physiological, physical and mental means, which let the intelligence of the cells respond to normal reactions.

Physiologically there are three means, requiring use of your intelligence.

First, provide bulk for the large intestine to act on. It is at least two inches in diameter. Unless bulky food is eaten, the muscle fibers of the intestinal walls soon get out of the habit of acting intelligently and lose the habit of moving the intestines regularly.

Bulky food must not be starchy. For a hundred years, we have eaten starch foods to give bulk. This pastes up the walls of the large intestine. Since its muscle fibers are less than 1/100th of an inch thick, they give up in despair and won't even try to move, if you plaster them with hard pasty wastes a half an inch thick.

The intestines must have bulk; yet it must not be loaded with hardened paste.

So, for bulk, instead of eating starch foods, eat green leaf products. Eat spinach, beet tops, lettuce, chard, celery, etc. These furnish vital vitamins and salts, also provide bulk which is not starchy.

Then use Agar-Agar. It can be purchased in packages or bought in bottles in form of liquid cream. It is made from a sea plant. It is a real vegetable wood. It can not ferment and does not putrify; but swells and produces bulk.

We have stretched the intestine for so many generations by use of so many fermenting and putrifying foods, that we must now give it bulk so that its muscle fibers will again use their intelligence. So, add Agar-Agar to your food. Use it as directed on the package, or on the bottles. It can be purchased at drug stores and in some grocery stores. It is not a medicine at all. It is a food.

As a second physiological means, use some lubricating foods, - a very little mineral fat. Mineral oils do not free as much acid as the animal and vegetable oils. Nujol is the best mineral oil. Take only about a half a teaspoonful a day. Do not take it to relieve constipation; take it as a lubricating food.

Third, physiologically, if you do not use many watery foods, drink distilled water.

"Water drinking, as we have seen, serves to facilitate elimination through the bowels by preventing the absorption of the colon poisons into the blood." (1)

There are also physical means which help. Many physical exercises have been given - twisting the body this way and that way, bending it forward and back.

In a course, which I wrote 30 years ago, I gave two such exercises. I do not repeat them here, for such exercises are of little value in curing constipation.

But what is of real value is freeing the circulation of the downward pull of organs in the abdomen. Walking around on all fours for two minutes morning and night, lets the intestinal tract hang as it should hang from its attachments at the back. This relieves all pressure of an over weighted intestine or organs underneath it. It also frees abdominal circulation, so that the walls of the intestine regain activity.

---

(1) "How to Live" by E. L. FISK, M.D.

Then the mind can be used as a mental means of curing constipation. It can form habits of frequent action. The mind can change habits even of organs usually not under the control of the will. It can do this by subconscious suggestion.

One can use his own mind to form the habit of frequent evacuations.

"Thousands of people pass through life content with but one movement in 24 hours. Modern medical science - puts the blame of most of our ills on this injurious habit." (2)

"Wild animals free themselves from food remnants several times each day." (3)

"So do young human beings before they learn civilized habits. Who ever heard of a healthy baby with only one movement per day?" (4)

Specialists agree that one intestinal movement a day is stagnation. Constipation is a habit of inactivity. We have actually developed it by repressing the intelligent impulse of the intestine to act when it desired to act.

We should still be socially considerate; yet, consciously and subconsciously, we can get back to the habit of more than one evacuation a day.

We can re-awaken activity of the muscular walls of the intestine, composed of millions of intelligent muscle fibers - each fiber composed of intelligent cells - much more intelligent than human beings.

Go to the stool at least three times a day. Do not strain but merely form the habit of going to the stool with the intention of evacuating the intestine.

The main thing is to establish the habit, with the intention of the mind, of restoring intestinal habits of evacuation at least three times every day.

Re-awaken the intelligence of intestinal cells - by use of brains, not brans.

Both nature curists and medical physicians advise bran. They claim that it stimulates the walls of the intestine. It does - just as I would stimulate you, if I should stand behind you jabbing you with ten thousand needles.

Look at a little bran under a microscope. It is composed of hard, razor like particles of the shell coverings of cereals. The tiny particles are almost as hard as glass. When they reach the intestine, they cut and scratch and tear. Then the thin intestinal walls call on the blood for help. The blood pours water into the intestine to wash these little pieces of vegetable glass out of the intestine.

Instead of bran, use brains.

————

(2,3,4) James Empringham, M.D. Health Education Society, N.Y.

Nothing will change a non-active deadened condition of the cells of the intestinal muscles, except action-impulses sent from your own soul to those cells.

To accomplish this, use each method given: one, to cleanse the intestine of impacted pasty wastes; another, to kill putrifying germs; another, to provide non-fermenting bulk; another, to free the intestine of poisons so that its muscle cells can act healthily. Then use your mind to re-establish habits of action.

And do not worry, for worry poisons cells and deadens their intelligence.

Perhaps there is no real constipation but only impaction and poisoning.

A great physiologist - one who has shown capacity for original thinking - says: "There are some cases of actual constipation, but usually it is a neurosis - a pattern idea of disease, deeply fixed to the mind of childhood." (5)

Mind habit - due to repression in childhood - due to repeated cautions not to allow the intelligence of the intestine to act except under restricted conditions - is the basic cause of lack of normal intestinal activity.

But mind habits can be changed; and bodily habits also.

———

(5) "The Human Body," by Logan Glendening, M.D.

BODY PURIFICATION

By
Brown Landone

LESSON XI - HOW TO HELP THE ORGAN WHICH BREAKS DOWN FIRST

What a god you are. Yes, in truth, you are a god - the one god of a world whose population is much more numerous than the human population of the whole earth.

In the United States, there are one hundred and fifty million people - men, women and children. Three times as many in India; three times as many in China.

Yet, the cells of your body - little individuals of which you are the god - number 54 million times as many as all the people in both China and the United States.

The little Red Indians of your blood number 30,000,000,000 to each spoonful. Also there are about 50 billion little white men in your blood.

None of these little individuals live more than 20 days. Within three weeks new born cells will take their place, and the wastes of the bodies of some 25 thousand billion red men, and of 50 billion white men must be carried out of your body.

This numbers only cells of your blood, which is but 7 pounds of your weight. The rest of your body contains many more thousands of billions of cells.

Other millions of billions have lived and died in your body in the last ten years; and as these little individuals passed on, they left the disintegrative wastes of their bodies behind, to be carried out of the body day by day.

Then there are other functional wastes of which the body must be purified.

The functions of the liver, for instance, are those of a chemical laboratory. It handles all proteins; changes vegetable sugar to animal sugar back to vegetable sugar; and whenever there is an extra amount of any substance, it has to store it away, or throw it into the blood as waste poison to be carried out of the body.

Then also there are emotive wastes - which for lack of a better term - I call emotive poisons; and, perhaps the term is wisely used after all.
For emotions do produce chemical changes in the body. Our chemistry is emotive, and our emotions are chemical. Every emotion which makes us more joyous and happy produces chemicals which can be used by the body. Every repression of an emotion produces another kind of chemical - a poisonous waste. Sometimes such wastes become very poisonous - some of them poisoning us almost unto death in a very short time.
When negative emotive attitudes become habits, the poisoning becomes chronic, lasting year after year, and making life almost impossible.

You are the god of the entire universe of the cells of your body, and they must live in whatever substances you create in your body.

If you create wastes due to repressed emotions, you saturate your blood with poisons, and the cells of your body are immersed in them and poisoned by them.

We have studied fatigue poisons; mineral wastes; acid crystals; poisonous acid bloat in between cells; physiological wastes packed in the intestine; and germs which develop in its fermenting cesspool. Now we add disintegrative wastes, functional wastes, and poisons due to repressed emotions.

If you free and purify the body of these, no one can say how long you may live in perfect youthfulness. Physiologists think it should be forever.

There are but two other means of purification for us to consider - that of drainage and that of breathing. So now we come to water and sunlight and air.

Purification by drainage is effected by the kidneys and the skin.
And purification by breathing is effected by the skin and the lungs.

The kidneys are of vital importance because they clean out such a great amount of wastes which, if left in the body for 48 hours, would poison us unto death.

"The kidneys are not glands of secretion; they secrete nothing. They are excretory organs. Their function is to filter from the 500 quarts of blood which flows through them every 24 hours - poisonous nitrogenous wastes, salts, and enough water to carry them in solution through the ureters to the bladder." (1)

"As the blood courses through - - the kidney-cells take up water, salts and wasted bodies (particularly the nitrogenous waste bodies such as urea, uric acid, creatinine, and creatin). All of these waste bodies result from the breakdown of albuminous or protein materials. The amonia urea, uric acid and creatinine are almost entirely the end products of food waste." (2)

"The creatin probably comes exclusively from the breakdown of the muscles." (3)

"After the kidney cells remove these substances from the blood, they are washed out of the tubules into the pelvis of the kidney, down the ureter into the bladder and then cast off by the act of urination." (4)

"Protein yields - - urea. This is a white crystalline substance in the pure form and roughly 90% of the nitrogen in protein metabolized by the body is excreted as urea. Other excretory substances containing the nitrogen of protein are uric acid, creatinine, and ammonia." (5)

"The process of urine secretion goes on constantly, at the rate of abou a drop every 30 seconds from each kidney." (about 86,400 drops a day). (6)

"Urine, then, is the means of excreting all the products of cell activity and nearly all abnormal substances that may at any time enter or be produced in the body." (7)

"The chief organs for such elimination are the kidneys." (8)

(1) "Why We Behave Like Human Beings" by G. A. Dorsey, Ph.D., L.L.D.
(2,3,4,6) "The Human Body" by Logan Glendening, M.D.
(5,7) "Physiology" by V. H. Mottram.
(8) "How to Live" by E. L. Fist, M.D.

The kidneys form the great purifying system of the body. Most of our physical troubles, old age, and death, are due to over-working them. Yet their normal activity can be re-established with just a little purification.

The skin also purifies the body by draining waste poisons from it.

The skin possesses a network of very small fibers running in all directions. Waste material, which is carried to the underlayer of the skin by the blood, is eliminated through pores. At the bottom of each pore is a sweat gland; and this is connected with a 'vegetative nervous system' which is the most vital nerve system in the body. That is why in the next Lesson I caution against 'nerve reactions' after baths.

"About 2,000,000 tiny pores - - - in our skin, about 500 the square inch, about 2,000 per s.quare inch in the palms of our hands and the soles of our feet." (9)

"There are two types of glands (the sweat glands and the oil glands) which pour out material on the surface of the skin. The sweat glands work in hot weather and their secretion is mainly water -- The oil glands secrete a waxy or icy material which coats the skin, makes it more resistant to water and more pliable, and is of advantage in the preservation of temperature." (10)

A very large amount of waste poison passes out through the skin's pores.

Even on a cold day in winter, a person doing ordinary work will excrete a pint of perspiration each 24 hours. Firemen and stokers on our large steamers often perspire three gallons per day.

Closing up the pores means death. In the early days of the church, it was the custom during church theatricals to have angels represented by boys and to gild the bodies of these boys for such sacred festivals. If they remained gilded for from three to ten days, the boys often became seriously ill and sometimes died.

Although during this time such boys were eliminating waste matter through the lungs, the kidneys, and the large intestine, yet the amount of poison retained because the pores of the skin were glazed with gold paint, was sufficient to cause death.

The skin with its marvelous structure breathes out poisons as well as drains off poisons in sweat. In this, it cooperates with the lungs.

The skin does an immense amount of work in purifying the body. In the next Lesson I will reveal to you one of the great secrets of my long active life, my ability to live and love and play and work 20 hours a day. It is the secret of the air bath, which is more important than either the water bath or the sun bath.

----

(9) "Why We Behave Like Human Beings" by G. A. Dorsey
(10) "Physiology" by V. H. Mottram, Professor Physiology, Univ. of London.

And the LUNGS: "Lungs are enormously complex sponges - minute pockets of air cells." (11) Combining the surface of the skin of all these pockets, gives us the total lung surface inside the body.

"Lung surface is from ninety to one hundred times greater than body surface. An average man has about one square yard of skin surface. About ninety square yards of lung surface." (12)
"Taking air is a vital process - in fact, no process is more vital."(13)

Of course, lungs are able to purify the body only because the blood brings the poisons of the body to the lungs from every corner of the body.
"Around it goes - - - the heartbeat forces it to keep moving. The vasomotor apparatus, through nerve connections with the muscle walls of the arterial system, controls the amounts of blood flow to the various tissues and organs of the body." (14)
The blood uses every one of its 25 thousand billion little red cells, especially designed to carry waste poisons from every nook of the body to the lungs.
Although there is only four quarts of blood in your body, yet since it circulates round and round, some 500 quarts pass by the air sacs of the lungs every 24 hours, and each spoonful of the 500 quarts contains 30,000,000,000 little red cells carrying poisons to the lungs to purify your body.

Their work is very important for they carry the most deadly poison in the body, carbon dioxide. No wonder we die in three or four minutes from accumulated poison, if purification by means of the breath is shut off.

There are several functions of breathing; purification is but one function.
In the next Lesson, I give particular means of breathing by the skin and lungs so that you will eliminate the wastes carried to skin and lungs.

But before closing this Lesson, learn what you can do to secure greater urification by that marvelous draining system - the draining system of the idneys.
Through them, 40 pints of blood are filtered every hour. A half ton, day.

The most serious danger in middle life is the breakdown of kidneys.
The breakdown results in poisoning and early death.
The breakdown is due to over-working the kidneys.

When we neglect the skin, it eliminates but half the impurities it should eliminate; then the kidneys must get rid of the rest. This over-works the kidneys.
When the intestines are constipated, poisons are absorbed into the blood; then the kidneys must drain these extra poisons from the blood.

———

(11,12,13,14) "Why We Behave Like Human Beings" - G. A. Dorsey.

When we do not breathe in the way which purifies the blood, the kidneys must assume the burden of poisons which should be eliminated by breathing.

What then can we do at once to help the kidneys in their purification work?

First, use all other purification methods, to lessen the burden on the kidneys.

Second, use more water - distilled water. "People who habitually have drunk too little water - - - often experience a remarkable increase of health and energy by attending systematically to this simple but important need." (15)

"People who neglect to drink sufficient water often show a urine of high density, 1,025 to 1,060, and suffer from symptoms of intestinal absorption. Headache, muscular and neuralgic pain, dullness, and lack of concentration are some of the symptoms of this condition." (16)

"In order to carry off the products of metabolism through the kidneys, large potations are needed." (17)

Third, use plenty of good tea and coffee.
"The rate of urinary flow may be increased by various agents. - - The best known are coffee and tea." (18)

Yes, coffee and tea - although once damned without reason - are very beneficial. We are learning new truths.

Not long ago, we thought the tomato was very poisonous. And under Dr. Wiley's regime in the U.S. Department of Agriculture, no one took trouble to determine the valuable mineral salts in foods. After determining starches, sugars, proteins, and fats, they burned everything else, and called it ashes.

With new knowledge, we know that coffee and tea greatly assist the kidneys, the most vital draining system of last resort, in purification of the body.

For more than 50 years, I have averaged 20 to 30 cups of coffee daily.

(15, 16) "How to Live" by E. L. Fisk, M.D.
(17) "Physiology" by V. H. Mottram
(18) "The Human Body" by Logan Glendening, M.D.

BODY PURIFICATION

By
Brown Landone

LESSON XII - THE BATH THAT GIVES YOU THREE EXTRA HOURS OF LIFE EACH DAY

If all purification by means of the kidneys is stopped, you die in three days.

If all purification by means of breathing is stopped, you die in three minutes.

So purification by breathing, by skin and lungs, is the most vital purification.

Of outside skin covering your entire body, there is only one square yard.

Of inside skin folded into lung air sacs, there is 90 square yards.

Your outside skin purifies by sweat drainage, and by breathing out vapors.

"A big tree will sweat a half-ton of water on a hot day." (1)

"An average man - - can sweat as much as ten pints; in that case 10% of his urea excretion would pass out through the sweat glands." (2)

Overworked kidneys are the greatest weakness of modern life; and real purification by skin can relieve overworked kidneys of one-tenth of their work.

The great problem is how to keep the skin's pores open and active, without making the skin sensitive to catching cold, and without causing a reaction of the skin nerves.

Study the three means in the order named - water bath, sun bath, and air bath.

Most people - even physicians - know little of the effects of water baths. Many claim that hot baths are weakening; others that cold baths are devitalizing.

An old man of ninety may assert that his long life is due to a cold bath every day for sixty years; and a dirty old 104 year old native of the Balkans might assert that his perfect health is the result of never having a bath in his life.

Many are so devitalized by cold baths, that they feel too stupid to think.

Others after taking a hot bath, become so sleepy that they cannot keep awake.

Everywhere people differ as to effects of hot and cold baths; some people, when tired and sleepy, are awakened and refreshed by a hot bath; others by a cold bath.

———

(1,2) "Why We Behave Like Human Beings" by G. A. Dorsey, Ph.D., LL.D.

There are many 'theories' and much ignorance of the whole subject of baths.

Hot Baths: The very hottest water bath known is that of the Japanese.
When an American traveler first takes a real Japanese bath, he thinks he is being scalded. Japanese for centuries have taken such hot baths frequently and regularly. Still they are a very enduring race. The hot bath has not weakened or devitalized them.

The Coldest Bath: The Russian peasants' bath of snow and ice water is the coldest bath of which I know. Early winter mornings, you can see children nude, outdoors washing themselves with snow, after which the mother dashes ice cold water over them.
It has not weakened the Russian peasants. They are a very enduring race.

These examples prove that we know little about the effects of water baths, which have more than one function. Some are to clean the skin - to wash off dirt; other baths are for purification (a) to help eliminate fatigue poisons by blood reaction, and (b) to keep pores open with nerve reaction.

Of course, if after a number of hours of physical work, your skin is dirty because of the large amount of poison excreted, or if you have been doing greasy or dusty work, then a warm or hot bath is necessary to clean the skin. The Turkish baths is not a true bath; it is a substitute for physical activity - for people too lazy to move enough to cause normal perspiration.

To understand why cold baths are so beneficial to certain people and detrimental to others, while hot baths are also beneficial to some people and detrimental to others, it is necessary to consider the habit of blood reaction in the body of the person who is taking the bath.

I was an invalid for the first 27 years of my life, and could not exercise enough physically to establish a habit of blood reaction from brain to muscles, and from muscles back to brain. But I studied 15 to 16 hours a day, so blood reaction was established between brain centers and internal organs.

My chauffeur, during his boyhood, was very active physically, either in play or in work - much more active physically than mentally. Consequently in his body, a different habit of blood reaction was established - from the brain centers to his muscles, and from the muscles back to brain centers.

Of course, all of us were physically active in childhood and youth. But what I mean by "habitual blood reaction being determined by much physical activity or lack of it" is whether the person as a child and youth used his muscles more than his brain, or used his brain more than muscles.

For the person who was very active physically during childhood and youth, the cold bath is now beneficial, either when his body is tired or the brain fatigued.

But for the person who did not establish a strong habitual blood reaction from brain to muscles, the hot bath is the more beneficial.

When you are very fatigued, you need a bath merely to change blood circulation - the hot bath if during childhood you were not very active physically; and the cold bath if during childhood you were physically very active.

Of course, the assumption that a cold bath brings blood to the muscles because it makes the skin glow, is ridiculously mistaken. When the skin glows it takes blood from the muscles to the skin. Also the assumption that a very hot bath - so hot that the skin becomes flushed - brings blood to the muscles, is mistaken. When skin becomes flushed, blood is taken from the muscles or from the brain. Yet, there is a .. water bath which a valuable means of purification.

The value of all water baths - except for washing the skin free of dirt - has been much over-emphasized. Any comparison with bath in the open as savages bathe when swimming - is no comparison at all, because the activity of swimming is the very opposite of the inactivity when in a bath tub.

Moreover, savages do not bathe much. The Red Indian has a beautiful skin of exceptional vitality - but how few water baths the Indian takes in a year.

Of course, a century ago, one could not exaggerate the value of the water bath; and its value today cannot be over-exaggerated for people living in slums or in far eastern countries of Europe. But in such cases, water baths qre needed as washings. (I've known people in the slums who had to be scrubbed to clean their skins).

But I am writing for you - for one who as a human individual does keep his skin reasonably clean, and so for you, I assert that the water bath has been over-used to such an extent that the skin has become almost non-active.

The skin of civilized man is degenerating. Skilled physicians who have become facial surgeons and beauty doctors know that much can be done with muscles of the face, but each great expert knows that he can never be certain that a skin operation or treatment will come successfully.

Once we thought of the skin with sweat pores, without recognizing the value of the oil glands. The oil glands secrete oil which protects the skin and feeds it. Too frequently water bathing today removes this oil, so the the skin is impaired.

Twenty years ago in Paris I met a woman of 65, one of the great beauties of Europe. When I asked her how she had kept her skin in such youthful condition, she told me that for years she had not taken a tub bath of more than two minutes at a time, and - immediately after each bath - she had used a cold cream such as actors used to clean the face of 'make-up'. Thus, she had cleaned her skin without depriving it of its own valuable oil; and the skin cells had been fed and had continued to grow new skin as creamy-pink and youthful as that of a child of ten.

"Removing sebaceous (oil) matter from the skin accompanied the downfall of Rome and Greece.

"New-born babies are washed in oil because it is found that washing in (warm) water - - - causes later, an abrupt fall in temperature. When washed in oil there is no such fall." (3)

"If you wash your feet frequently with water, or water and soap, a day's march is sure to blister them, unless you replace the oil you have washed out." (4)

"Scientists point out that pari passu with the ancient civilization love of the bath went their decadence." (5)

Too much water bathing is detrimental. Tub baths do not bathe - they soak.

Even animals which live in water, cover themselves with a water proof leather, or with scales, to prevent water from soaking into the skin.

Soaking the skin deadens the normal action of the skin. Skin was made for breathing - not be soaked. All soaking causes the pores to close up in a very short time after one is out of the water, and that keeps poisons in the body.

The one great problem of purification is to awaken the skin to greater activity, without causing nerve reactions which close the pores.

For this purpose, I many years ago evolved the Eliminative Bath - the Water Purification Bath. Because it keeps the pores of the skin open for 24 hours, it is to be taken once every day as follows:

FIRST: sponge the skin with warm water in which you have dissolved Epsom Salts - a teaspoonful to each quart of water used. Sponge yourself; keep in motion; have no one aid you in this. Doing it yourself helps normal circulation by means of your muscular activity.

I suggest sponging the body instead of soaking it in a tub. "Sponging" means using either a sponge or a cloth to wash the water over the body. Personally, I prefer a wet cloth. The sponge bath does not soak the skin in water; and it keeps you active. Moving to wash your body from heels to head, the whole body is active. Water baths should be taken with muscular activity. That is why swimming is beneficial, but too many tub baths detrimental.

(3,4,5) Physiology, p 227 - by V. H. Mottram.

SECOND, follow with either a cold spray or shower, or a cold sponge bath of clear water if you prefer sponging instead of spray or shower.

Third, gently rub the skin dry with your own hands. This may take three or four minutes - but it will give you an extra hour of life each day. Drying the skin with the palms of the hands, warms the skin, brings blood to it, dries it by the normal process of evaporation, and prevents any nerve reaction in the skin. (It may be necessary for a man with a hairy chest or limbs to use a towel on such parts before drying the body by rubbing with his hands as directed above.)

FOURTH, after you have rubbed the skin dry with your hands, step on a dry rubber mat, such as you can buy in any store which sells bath-room supplies.

FIFTH, standing on the mat, rub the skin gently and rapidly with a silk cloth, about a yard of uncolored pongee, or any good sized piece of white or cream colored silk.
This silk should be dry, and the body should be dry before using the silk. Then the skin will be given a treatment of frictional electrification which will make the pores remain open for 24 hours and prevent any nerve reaction.

AS TO THE SUN BATH: its great value is not in purifying the body but in producing re-growth within the body. Sunlight on the skin produces chemical changes which help to develop a very marvelous vitamin within the body. Sunlight is a magical cure for diseases of the bones, and hence very beneficial in revitalizing the marrow of the bones where red blood cells grow.
"Sun baths - continuous exposure of the skin to the sun as practiced in the Alps by Rollier - have a positively beneficial effect upon the whole system, flooding the deep organs with health and curing tuberculosis of the bones and joints." (6)
"These same rays (light) - - get into our skin - - they will paralyze an amoeba in a quarter of a second, or kill and tear its body assunder like a bolt of lightning in three seconds." (7)

So, too much sun bathing - making a fad of sun baths - is detrimental. Every form of life protects itself from too much exposure to the sun. Otherwise there would be no foliage on the earth and no hair on any animal except that which is grown as fur for protection from extreme cold. God and nature have tried to protect man from the sun. Hair was grown to protect both man's head and body - to protect the skin from the continuous exposure to the sun's rays.

(6) "The Human Body", p 68 by Logan Glendening, M.D.
(7) "Why We Behave Like Human Beings" by G. A. Dorsey, p 144.

USE the sun bath - to keep up the vitality of the bones; but not as an important means of purification - unless your skin is diseased and scabby.

REMEMBER: One-half of the time usually given to sleep is used in eliminating waste poisons. Many such poisons may be freed from the body by keeping the pores open. After a hot tub soak, a hot shower, or Turkish bath the nerves of the skin will react, and the pores of the skin close tight within two hours. This Water Purification Bath keeps pores open for 24 hours.

No other water bath gives you three extra hours each day.

But certainly you will not gain three extra hours the first day you take this bath, because only day by day will it help to eliminate more and more and more of the poisons already in the body. And, certainly, do not try to cut down your hours of sleep. Purify your body and sleep as much as you wish. Then gradually, as the body becomes purified, you will need less and less sleep, month by month.

The Water Purification Bath of this Lesson is one of the most beneficial means. It keeps the pores open 24 hours a day. Use it every day.

In the next lesson I give the Air Bath - for the skin was made for breathing - and the emotive purification breath to free the body of emotive poisons.

By
Brown Landone

LESSON XIII - BATH OF AIR AND THE BREATH OF LOVE

The skin of a sponge acts as a stomach, and soaks in food from water.
But the skin of the human body is made for breathing, not for a stomach.

Most poisons eliminated by the skin are breathed out as vapor. That
is why the skin will not sweat unless its breathing fails to reduce heat of
the body sufficiently.
The outer skin of your body breathes. So does the inner skin of your
lungs.
When you soak the skin of your lungs with water you stop its breathing
and drown breathing for the time, and make the lungs overwork to throw off
the waste poisons which should be breathed out by the skin.
Soaking your outside skin is not fatal because 90 square yards of
lung skin can do the work of one-square yard of outer skin; but soaking
the lungs is fatal because one yard of outer skin can not do all the work
done by 90 yards of lung skin.

"Some strange things about it (the skin) have been pointed out
recently - - - it has intimate connections with the vegetative nervous
system which controls or adjusts all the functions of the internal organs." (1)

Only lately have we recognized the extraordinary importance of the
connection of vegetative nervous system with the skin. The vegetative
system consists of ganglia "strung along the spinal column outside the
spinal canal - - it is the oldest part of the nervous system - - and it
is by all odds the most independent - - it sends fibres to all the organs,
beginning with the eye and salivary glands, clear down to the rectum and
bladder and womb - - (and) - - to the glands of perspiration." (2)

Since the vegetative nervous system is connected with the glands of
erspiration in the skin, every condition of the pores reacts on the
egetative nervous system and on all internal organs, even the ductless
lands - the miracle glands of life. That is why I emphasize the deadening
effect of soaking the skin in water.

When the skin's two million little outside lungs breathe freely, they
free the body of great quantities of waste poison, and cause the entire
vegetative nervous system to respond, affecting even ductless glands -
very controllers of life of the body.

The skin is a breathing surface; that is why the air bath is much
more beneficial than the water bath - hot or cold - shower, tub, or spray.

(1,2) "The Human Body" p 68, 204 by Logan Glendening, M.D.

After the water purification bath as given in the last lesson - or at any other convenient time - take the air bath of the gods.

The air bath is merely letting the air play freely on the naked body.

FIRST, for at least a half hour night and morning, expose the skin to air. It carries away all vapor poisons and even the water poisons sweated out of the skin. Unless the skin is dirty with grease, a half hour of air cleans it more than four hours in a tub bath. Water baths may soak wastes into the skin; air baths carry them away.

"How can your hands and feet and the rest of your skin breathe, if you do not let them repeatedly come in contact with the fresh air?" (3)

SECOND, air your underclothes at night. Turn them inside out, and shake them just as a farmer's wife shakes crumbs from a table cloth. Or, if you have an electric fan, hang the underclothes in the breeze of the electric fan for a few moments.

"WHEN YOU GET TIRED FROM YOUR WORK AT NIGHT, TRY THE EFFECT OF LAYING OFF EVERY GARMENT YOU HAVE ON AND DONNING FRESH ONES, AND SEE IF IT DOES NOT REST YOU. Let the fact that it permits increased oxidation of the blood by way of the skin, with a corresponding escape of carbonic acid gas, serve as an explanation, for it will be in conformance with what is really the case." (4)

THIRD, air bed sheets, every day - it is much more important than sunning them.

FOURTH, if the room is too cool to take a complete air bath, strip your body, and walk around, or busy yourself with work, clad only in a loose robe and slippers.

For the first few weeks, the room should be warmer than the usual temperature of rooms in which you live when dressed. Then little by little your skin will become accustomed to air and the air on your body will feel the same as air on your face.

More and more as I study how each form of life lives, I realize that mud is the bath for worm forms of life; that water is the bath for fish forms; that sunlight is the bath for lizards and alligator forms of life; and that air is the bath for men and gods.

The air bath will give you more energy, more youthful ness, and more additional hours of life for work and play and joy, than any other means of purification.

And now emotions - and freedom from the very poisons of soul inactivity - the deadly destructive poisons produced in the body by repressed emotions.

I doubt, however, if there is any such condition as a negative emotion, although there are negative effects of repressed emotions.

---

(3) "The Composite Man", p 98, by E. H. Pratt, A.M., M.D., Ll.D.
(4) Ibid.

"Motion" means movements, and "E" means outward. An emotion is the outward movement of the soul.

Mind perceives and takes in what it gains by contact with the outer world. But love or emotion gives out of itself; and forever continues to give out.

The great emotion is love; it gives of its life - "It thinketh not of itself."

EXPRESSED emotions are those feelings which aid not only the physiological functions of the body but gives us all the happiness and joy of living.

Repressed emotions retard our activities, and chemically poison our bodies.

Every emotion is good, but any good emotion may be repressed until its effect is negative or destructive. This is true of all powers.

Steam for instance has power of expansion. Every true expression of steam is of benefit to man. But if steam is enclosed in a boiler - with all the valves closed, and fires kept burning - there will come a time when its expansion will cause the boiler to explode. But the steam cannot be called evil or negative. It is those who do not allow proper outlet for use of the steam who are at fault.

It is not steam which is evil, but the repression of the steam.

So with emotions. Individuals of those races who love most are also the individuals most torn with hate and jealousy when their love is repressed.

Love seeks expression. If this expression is prevented - if the person who is loved does not return the love but loves another, then the love of the first finds no outlet in expression, and his repressed love may become hate.

Repressed courage becomes fear - thus the person who always expresses courage cannot possibly have fear for nothing of courage is repressed; repressed mirth and joy become sadness and sorrow, et cetera.

Hence, it is better to classify emotions as expressed and repressed emotions. /not

It is/the emotion, but the repression of the emotion which poisons the body, unbalances the mind, and tears the soul asunder in agony.

All expressed emotions produce chemicals which sustain and endure.

All repressed emotions produce chemicals which poison the tissues of the body.

Repressed emotions also change the chemistry of blood, breath, tears, saliva, gastric juice, urine, bile, perspiration, and sex fluids.

"It cannot be emphasized too much that - - - shame fills our cheeks with blood. Fear drives the blood away. Excitement quickens the heart-beat. Grief brings tears." (5)

"Sighs cause disturbances of regular breathing. A great shock to the mind may cause fainting, the rush of blood from the head into the abdomen. Worry will interfere with digestion and sleep. The X-Ray has detected the arrest of the persistaltic movement of the stomach and intes-tines because of a strong emotion." (6)

"Strong emotion may lead to a great increase in the sugar in the blood, sometimes enough to cause its appearance in the urine as though the person had diabetes." (7)

"Cannon, Crile, and others have shown that pain, hunger, anger and fear, influence the secretion of the adrenal glands above the kidneys, causing the release of sugar in the blood and the experience of fatigue." (8)

"An insurance doctor always should test the urine of the clients - - suppose grape sugar appears, it may mean merely that the patient has had a large bag of sweets - - or it may be the result of fear of the examination. Substitutes in an important football game in the U.S. although they never took part in the game, showed grape sugar in the urine." (9)

Each repressed emotion produces a chemical. Such a poison produced in one animal produces a like condition when injected into the blood of another animal.

In great fear, cold perspiration carries the extra poison from the body; in great anger, upper lobes of the lungs actually pant, to get rid of the poison.

In a few moments intense jealousy may poison fluids in the liver so that the person becomes jaundiced for life. Intense grief may paralyze tear glands so that weeping is impossible; great fear may stop the heart to instant death.

It is not the explosion of repressed emotions which are most detrimental although they show up the worst - it is the continued suppressed emotions week after week, year after year - which produces the continuous poisoning.

But there is a way out. As repressed emotions produced poisons, so expressed emotions produced chemicals which result in approximate eternal youth.

The boy who is very tired sawing wood, becomes refreshed by a game of ball. Grown-ups, physically tired, spend half the night dancing, and are physically refreshed. The chemicals produced by expressed emotions counteract the poisons of repression.

(5, 6, 7, 8) "How to Live" by E. L. Fisk, M.D.
   (9) "Physiology" by V. H. Mottram.

The law of the vital activity of life is so simple, we usually over-look it. It is this: opposing activities cannot take place at the same time. You cannot breathe in while breathing out. You cannot go back-wards while you are going forward.

So also, you cannot repress an emotion while expression of the emotion takes place. You can not feel hungry while expressing love; or repress emotions when you are freely using the middle lobes of the lungs, awakening the emotive brain to greater expression.

In Lesson II, I taught you the Purification Breath - how to breathe to remove three times as much fatigue poison per minute as is done in ordinary breathing.

NOW I give you another mode of breathing - the Love Breath of God.

It is sufficient to know (a) that the lungs are composed of five lobes, (b) that different lobes are neurally related to different brain centers, (c) that the middle lobes are supplied by nerve fibres which form great trunk lines and connect indirectly with the solar plexus brain - that is, with the emotive brain.

Hence, when you function the middle lobes of the lungs, your breath-ing re-awakens the solar plexus brain which is the emotional brain of the body and compels emotional expression. Expression neutralizes the waste poisons of repressed emotions.
This is the emotive breath I give you, and since it is the Love Breath, and since God is Love, I dare to call it the Love Breath of God.

First, place one hand on each side directly over lower ribs where they can be expanded most easily. Place hands with palms against the body, the fingers forward.

Second, breathe in easily for seven counts with a feeling of calmness and quiet love; then breathe out for seven counts with a feeling of mirth and joy - seven counts for in-breath, seven counts for out-breath, repeating seven times.

Third, breathing easily in and out, try to feel angry. You cannot. You cannot even feel annoyed. As you begin breathing rhythmically with this breath of love, repressed feelings must begin to vanish. You cannot repress when you are expressing.

Fourth, practice this breathing so often, that within four or five months, it will become a habit - your habitual mode of breathing. Your emotive outlook on life will be changed. That is the most important thing in the world. But, in addition, this will completely change the chemistry of your body, continually creating chemicals which give vitality and buoyancy and youthfulness to the cells of the body.

I have not needed as much sleep as most people, because when I was seventeen, I had to purify my body of mineral and acid wastes in order to live. That taught me a great lesson. Year by year I have learned additional means of purification.

Men usually work from eight to nine hours a day - physically or mentally. For half a century I have averaged twice as much - at least eighteen hours a day. Hence, in actual living, I have enjoyed a hundred years during the last fifty years of my life.

What I have done, you can do. This course includes what I have used. Use it.

You must purify or grow old and die. Purification of the cells means almost physical immortality as proved by Dr. Carrel's work in keeping the cells alive, merely by continually washing away the waste poisons produced by their activities.

God's Law holds - each produces after its own kind; pure thinking produces a pure mind; pure living, a pure character; and purification of body, a pure body.

Each is necessary. During the last 20 years, four great spiritual leaders have passed on. No one can doubt their purity of ideas, purity of heart, purity of living. Yet, one died of wasted cell structure; another of poisoned lung tissues; the third of intestinal poisons; and the fourth of acid bloat. Yet, each had realized the Truth of spiritual life and declared that his or her body would never die.

We need but one thing more. In addition to purity of thought, purity of feeling, and pure living, we need purity of body. With that, what may we not attain?

Physiologically, Carrel proves that cells have eternal youth if kept purified of the wastes which they produce; spiritually, Christ taught purity of thought as eternal life; practically, we have the privilege of demonstrating both.